MISSING IN THE WOODS

Steph Young

Copyright 2018 Steph Young
All Rights Reserved

People are going missing in the wilderness.

Something in the woods is taking people. Something unknown that we cannot define; something that others have had the misfortune to encounter.

People are snatched soundlessly, never to be seen again. Or they are returned; dead.

Strange and highly unusual predators are in the woods. Highly intelligent. Very successful. And able to overpower someone in an instant.

This is a puzzle. A deadly one. People are going missing in the woods. Here follow some very troubling and disturbing true accounts....

Table of Contents

Introduction 5

Chapter One: The Disappeared 7

Chapter Two: Into the Bayou 16

Chapter Three: Missing Doctors, Missing Scouts 37

Chapter Four: Missing Children, Missing Rangers 61

Chapter Five: More Vanishing Children 80

Chapter Six: Missing Hunters 90

Chapter Seven: More Strange Disappearances 102

Chapter Eight: "POSSE SEEKING MISSING WOMAN."128

Chapter Nine: GONE 138

Chapter Ten: Missing Genius 148

Chapter Eleven: Strange Encounters 163

Chapter Twelve: Isle of Mull Disappearance 207

Excerpt from Lured in the Woods 242

Introduction

Fatal accidents can happen very easily to even the most experienced of hikers or climbers. In the wilderness, hikers can get lost in an instant. A couple of wrong turns and they can be lost immediately, unable to know which direction to proceed in, and very quickly the panic can set in. A slip on a rock or a trip near a crevice, and death or serious accidents can come fast.

When falling into a creek, a ravine or between a pile of rocks, a body dead or injured, can be hidden from search parties quite easily. However, with highly trained tracker dogs, professional search and rescue teams and heat seeking infra-red equipment to detect a person's body heat, the mystery often remains as to why some people are not found, or, why they are found in the most unusual and sinister of circumstances.

Natural predators can lurk in the wilderness; bears, mountain lions, cougars, and occasionally a hiker will be victim to these wild animals. They feed where they kill or drag their bloody victim to a nearby lair; they leave a trail that is obvious to searchers.

However, the victims in this book show no evidence of an animal attack. For these victims, there is no logical explanation.... only cryptic mysteries, enigma and many unanswered questions...

People in the Woods are disappearing....

People are being taken; sometimes they are returned, but they are never the same again....

Something in the woods is taking people. Something unknown that we cannot define; something that others have had the misfortune to encounter.

People are snatched soundlessly, never to be seen again. Or they are returned; dead.

Chapter One

The Disappeared

Melvin Nadel was on a hunting trip with friends. He told them he was going to head down trail by approximately 150 yards to hunt there. He had once got lost before, and this had made him extra cautious. He did not like to head too far away from camp. He also had an injured knee and so could not go too far due to the discomfort this caused him.

It was September 6th, 2009, and Melvin and his two friends were hunting in the Elk Mountain area of the Santa Fe National Forest near Pecos, New Mexico. He carried with him a .44 revolver along with his bow and arrow. It was around 4.30 pm when he left his two friends to walk the 150 yards. He said he'd be back before dark. He never returned.

His jeep was still there, parked beside the camp with his

gear inside including his cell phone, backpack and GPS. Usually he would take the GPS with him, but perhaps he thought it was completely unnecessary given that he would only be a few yards away from camp.

At the time of his disappearance he owned a Gym in Santa Fe, New Mexico. He was very fit and also held a black belt in tae kwon do. His hunting style was said to be the long-wait rather than actively hunting. He was married with a daughter who was enrolled at a local college. His wife said she knew of no health problems and she knew no reason why he would disappear. She didn't believe he would willingly leave them.

When tracker dogs were brought in they followed his scent for 100 yards along the trail. Police could find no signs of foul play. All they could presume was that he must have wondered off and got lost and then got stranded.

His brother-in-law was one of the two men who'd gone hunting with him. They'd camped close to the logging road. When they separated at 4.30 pm, the other two men went along the trail and into the forest, while Nadel stayed very close to their camp.

The two men returned at around 7pm but saw no sign of him at the camp. They searched all around but found no evidence of him, yet his jeep was still parked there. They said they called out for him but never got an answer. They even honked their horns for him, and then fired their guns, to try to alert him to their concern. As the hours went by, they began to get increasingly worried.

It was then that they turned to the authorities. Although they were concerned he was lost, his two companions were not overly worried about his safety at this point given that he was a black-belt, had a hunting knife and carried a gun; it was fairly obvious he could look after himself, if necessary.

His search turned into the biggest search in the State's history. The search was huge, and it involved hundreds of volunteers, trained search and rescue personnel, teams of dogs, ATV's, and helicopters. The man's tracks were followed, and his scent, but it inexplicably stopped abruptly at approximately 100 yards from camp.

There, the dogs became confused and unable to know which direction to proceed in. They couldn't find which way his scent went – they couldn't pick up his scent anymore. His footprints just stopped. There was nothing else there – no sign of a struggle, no blood, no ripped clothes, no animal tracks, no vehicle tracks, no spent shells.

One strange theory developed; that the man had run off with a fancy-woman and left his family behind, staging his disappearance perhaps by back-tracking over his own footprints, and running off. But how? - His jeep was still there, there were no other vehicle tracks, and he certainly couldn't have run anywhere with a bad knee. His scent also couldn't be tracked.

A pair of brand-new women's jeans had been found in his jeep, giving rise to this theory, and yet his wife appeared completely unconcerned about the possibility of this being credible in any way. She explained that because he was not a tall man, he bought whatever jeans would fit him and if those were women's jeans he couldn't have cared less.

His bank cards were never touched after that day either, and he would have been leaving behind a very successful business and his daughter. He was never known to have any enemies either. Mel's wife, Edna said, "People just don't disappear," but bizarrely in this case, it seems they do.

Search and Rescue Crews found no clues in their search for him. His wife said, "Whatever happened to my husband, we need to find out," after searchers had spent yet another day scouring the wilderness for him. His daughter said, "I honestly don't think he just got lost." Search crews had been looking for him for a week. "No signs, no leads" said authorities. Even black hawk helicopters were used in the search for him.

"It's just like a bubble – 'Puff' and they're gone," said

his wife, "And I ask them, how are they going to explain this to me? I have a lot of questions but get no answers – nobody can answer my questions..."

Approximately 5 miles away from where Nadel vanished into thin air, so too did an elderly lady. 71-year-old Emma Tresp vanished en-route to a religious retreat. All that remains of her is a small statue marking the spot where she disappeared. It's a tiny statue of an angel and a cross, on the spot where her car was found.

It's reported that her footprints were found circling her car but there was no sign of her at all. No scent could be tracked and no sign of her could be found. She'd abandoned her car on a dirt road. It was not a road she should have been heading down. It was not a road that would take her to her retreat.

It was in rural New Mexico, on August 31st, 1998 and it was only a few miles from where Nadel had disappeared. This healthy and well and active mother had left her daughter's home in Stillwater, Oklahoma on a road trip to Pecos where she would join a retreat at the Benedictine Monastery. She had been to the Monastery on retreat several times before and so this was a route that was somewhat familiar to her.

She had been driving alone and had last been seen stopping at a gas station in the town of Santa Rosa, where she filled up with gas and it was captured on the security footage. After that, her car was discovered down a rural forestry road 63A, near the Glorieta and Pecos. Locally, the road is known under a different name; Camino Del Diablo, or The Devil's Road. Her car was said to have been lodged on a rock.

The most reasonable explanation was that she must have left her car to seek aid, willingly walking away from her car without her cell phone to get help, having got her car stuck on the rock; but no-one could explain why she would have taken that forestry road in the first place.

The road is a rough unpaved road in the middle of a heavily wooded area in the Santa Fe National Forest, that no car driver would wish to drive down. The damage done to the car would not be worth it, and, it was not a route to anywhere other than into the deep forest.

Certainly, it would not look like an appealing or sensible choice for a careful woman in her seventies. To get to the Monastery from Interstate 25, she should have taken State Highway 63. When her car was found, it was locked and the forest road it was on, was approximately 15 miles from Route 63 where she should have been.

Her daughter is Sister Rose Marie Tresp. "Her car was located, but neither she nor her purse was found despite extensive searching by the New Mexico Search and Rescue Team and local police, a private detective, and the FBI took DNA samples." There was "Extensive publicity, and even consultations with psychics. There was no success," says her daughter. She had been to the Monastery several times before and was familiar with the route to get there. For some unfathomable reason, her car ended up down a remote forestry road, way off her route.

When the searchers began to look for her, after a hunter had come across her abandoned car, her footprints circled the car but none of her footprints actually led away from the car, which is most peculiar. There also didn't appear to be any other person's footprints there, indicating that it did not appear anyone else had been there with her.

The experienced trackers were unable to find a direction to go in; they had nothing to follow. Also, it was reported that the tracker dogs were not able to pick up her scent. They too had nothing to go on. It was as if she had never left her car at all, other than to walk around it, and yet, where was she? And how could she have disappeared when there was no scent nor any footprints leading away from the car?

No other fingerprints were found inside the car, or outside. There was no sign of a struggle inside or outside the car.

As State Police investigator David Martinez said, "It's like she vanished off the face of the Earth ….There are no answers."

Chapter Two

Into the Bayou

The strange tale of a man's disappearance involving Silver Elves, a Hitman in a Cadillac, an Elvis impersonator, and a home invasion. In December 1998, 23-year-old Matthew David Pendergrast was in his last semester at Rhodes College, Tennessee.

On the morning he disappeared, he'd been due at class, a distance of four blocks away from his apartment. He left his apartment in Memphis, Tennessee, but he never arrived at class, and he has never been seen since. That same day, his Toyota vehicle was found abandoned on a private levee near Bayou Meta swamp, off Kerr Road in Lanoke County, Arkansas, off Interstate 40.

This area was private land reserved for duck hunters. One of the hunters who found the vehicle, Joe Murdall, told Matthew's mother Mary Ellen that he and a friend had seen her son's SUV parked up there at around 2 pm. He said it had not been there when they'd passed the area at 10 am that morning.

They'd left a note on the windshield, asking for the owner of the vehicle to move it. The next day, they saw that the vehicle was still there, and it was then that they looked inside it for some i.d. The keys were still in the ignition and it was unlocked. In the glove compartment, they found an old oil change receipt that had Matthew's parent's home phone number on it.

The vehicle was unlocked, and the keys were inside. So too was the backpack he used for college. During a search of the area around the car the following day, his wallet containing his driver's license, credit card and $46 in cash, was found inside his jean's pocket, approximately 100 yards from his abandoned vehicle in a wooded thicket.

His clothes were also found in the woods there, in a pile; blue jeans and a t-shirt, as well as his shoes and socks. But there was no sign of Matthew.

He had seemingly driven way-off course that morning, driving approximately 125 miles, then turning off the highway and driving down a private dirt road to a levee and swamp. He'd taken his shoes and all his clothes off, and vanished, or so it would appear.

By all accounts, his pants were wet from the knees down, as though he had stepped out of them and dropped them to the floor where he stood – yet, they were found in a wooded area of thickets. Although his pants were soaking, according to one of the investigators on the scene, his T-shirt was as dry "as if it had just come out of the dryer." Although it was winter, no jacket was found.

As for the rest, or as much of what is known of the rest of the story, it will involve the curious and often inexplicable actions of a cast of characters including silver Elves, a Hitman in a Cadillac, an Elvis impersonator, and a home invasion.

Matthew was last seen leaving his residence in Memphis between 7:30 a.m. and 8:00 a.m. on December 1,

2000, in his SUV which had Georgia license plates. His landlady heard him moving around just before this.

The previous evening, he had appeared in a play on campus. After that, back at his apartment, he had called a friend in Atlanta to discuss what he would write in an upcoming college paper. His friend, Geo Presley-Brookes said he was upbeat when they'd talked. Early the following morning he'd sent a text to the same friend saying; "Everything's all right. No problem. I'll talk to you later."

Some wonder, what did this message mean? Was it some kind of clue about what had happened to him, or what he was planning to do? And yet, probably the most obvious answer is that he had continued working on his planned college paper or run it through in his mind the night before, after speaking to his friend, and was now sure how he would write his college paper; so he was letting his friend know.

Matthew was slim and five feet six inches. He played in the college soccer team and had wrestled at the private school he'd attended in Atlanta. He liked to play tennis. He ran track and cross-country. He was sociable and well-liked. At college he joined the Kappa Sigma fraternity. He enjoyed playing a Multi User Dungeons and Dragons game online called Threshold-RPG.

When his parents received the call from the two hunters about his abandoned vehicle, they immediately began to co-ordinate a search from their home in Georgia. First, they phoned the college campus security.

Security checked his apartment and then issued an email to all students asking for anyone who knew his whereabouts to contact them. Over the next few days, searches were carried out for the missing student at the bayou. Helicopters flew over the swamp and woods with night vision, divers with sonar entered the water, and blood-hounds then cadaver dogs were brought in.

The K-9 team picked up the young man's scent from the pile of clothes to the edge of Bayou Meto. The search focussed on the thick woods and the water. Bayou Meto is a huge state-owned wildlife management area, comprising 30,000 acres and much of it is flooded. The river is a complex waterway that winds through five Arkansas counties. Beside the bayou is thick woodland.

Matt was never known as a camper or hiker. His parents and the investigators could see no obvious attraction for Matt to be here.

Strangely, although the dogs picked up the young man's scent from the pile of clothes to the edge of Bayou Meto, the dogs found no scent to follow from his vehicle to his clothes. There were also no footprints. Investigators also found no signs of a struggle, no weapons, nor any DNA evidence. How did this all seem possible?

The tracker dogs could only intermittently pick up on his scent, and some of the investigators even wondered if he had actually made it to the spot where his car and clothes were found. When his clothing was found, his mother expressed the opinion that it appeared to be possible that this was staged – her son, she said, was not particularly neat and tidy, so she couldn't imagine him placing his clothes down in such a neat pile. His bedroom at home was notoriously untidy, she explained, so she did not feel this was the work of her son.

On the other hand, a very strange commonality of suicide victims who kill themselves by walking into rivers or the sea is often that they will strip naked and place their clothes on the shore in a very orderly neat and tidy pile before wading into the water.

Could he have taken his own life? Perhaps, although the divers found no body. He was also described as being "upbeat" during his phone call in the early hours before he disappeared, had been in a play the night before, and was planning a paper he was due to write. He was sociable, had friends and would seem to have had no problems that could have led him to be suicidally depressed.

His mother said, "He was a little worried about papers he had due you know, to finish up his degree, but other than that he was in good spirits. He was an excited young man who was looking forward to graduating. He had plans of starting his own non-profit organization to help those in need in Third World countries. So, he was looking forward like he had a bright future, with direction and meaning in his life. If Matt were interested in some type of respite or retreat, he would have gone to the mountains. We were unaware of any knowledge he might have had of this particular area."

One strange clue however did lead investigators to contemplate suicide though. As already mentioned, when he was not studying or playing soccer or tennis, he took great enjoyment in playing the interactive online fantasy game of 'Dungeons and Dragons,' and this online game had a curious link to something found in his abandoned car.

A journal discovered inside Matthew's car contained poetry he had written. The poems were contemplations on life and nature and death, with some entries describing 'The Silver Elves.' He wrote about 'Silver Elves' and seeking immortality, and about "walking into water and becoming one with nature again." It's unclear what he meant in these writings; whether he was being creative or literal. His parents said that there was no way he would simply walk into the water and drown himself.

And yet, cryptically the online game he played a lot had a link to the website; 'The Silver Elves.' This was where the words he had written in his journal had come from. The link led to a website for a group called 'The Silver Elves' and featured 'The Elven Tree of Life and Death.'

The website explained, 'The Silver Elves are a family of elves who have been living and sharing the Elven Way since 1975,' and if you choose, you can go on 'A journey; The Elven Tree of Life Eternal, known to men as the Tree of Life and Death reveals the pathways to Faerie and the means to obtaining Immortality, which some seem to think is the doom of the Elves even while they hunger after it.'

They say, 'The journey begins here... We start here at the bottom of the tree, the ever-present NOW. This is the place of the earth, symbolized by the cross (time/space) in the circle (eternity)."

The mysterious group offers you the chance to discover if you are 'an Elf, Faerie, or Otherkin,' and says, 'We will share with you the philosophy, magic and lifestyle of being elven. Elfin is like a secret garden in the midst of the wild and potentially dangerous realm that is Faerie. You are perfectly safe in Elfin but it may take a great deal of courage to pass through Faierie to get there.'

This strongly reminds me of the true tragic tale of Netty Fornario, who also went in search of the Faery realm only to be found dead on the moors on the barren Island of Iona; her bare feet clean but her toes bloodied and her face a death-mask of terror. She'd been trying to make contact with the faery realm, despite the stern warnings of her wise occultist friends of the danger it would put her life in.

And that is why her death reminded me of Matthew Predergrast's unexplained disappearance and of his writings about the Silver Elves, which according to reporter Marilyn Sadler of Memphis Magazine, there was one entry in his journal, found in his abandoned vehicle, in which he described 'the cold mud in the woods, lying down in the icy water, and feeling his blood turning to ice crystals.'

After finding the journal, the Lanoke County Sheriff's department decided to hire a psychic, Carol Pate, to assist them. Perhaps Matthew really had taken the twisted treacherous journey to what he thought would lead to immortality through drowning his body.

'The psychic claimed that he wanted to be rebirthed as a Silver Elf. The psychic said she "saw" Matt take off his clothes, fold them neatly, and step out into the bayou, where he died of hypothermia.' In other words, he didn't drown himself, but simply passively lay down to die in the cold mud.

She told KATV in a later interview that she believed Matthew "felt that he was in a battle for his soul, that he was battling demons and he lost."

However, his mother and his closest friends all said that he would never do a thing so crazy as to willingly wade into the water or mud at a random spot off a Highway and lay down there to die. His family didn't believe he would have taken his own life, and there was also no evidence that he was ever a drug taker.

His friend Jason Woods told Memphis Magazine, talking about the journal entries Matthew had made; "He wrote creatively about all aspects of life. Focusing on dark poems or fantastical ideas only sensationalizes and creates a non-sensical mystery. Give Matt privacy of thought and a modicum of respect." In other words, his friend's opinion was that it was a ludicrous suggestion and disrespectful to imply that Matthew would literally do anything he wrote in his journal – it was poetry, not reality, he firmly believed.

The Authorities searched for a week after his neat pile of clothes were found. Searchers came up with nothing however – no clues at all to explain where Matt was. All they could do was try to come up with ideas and theories. Lonoke County Sheriff investigator Jim Kulesa believed it was possible the clothes had been staged, and this could have been the case, given that Matthew's scent did not track from his vehicle to his clothing. But staged by who? And why?

His parents had to wonder, had he been kidnapped? Yet no ransom note ever came. The police suggested a carjacking, giving a ride to a hitcher which turned bad, or a drug deal gone wrong, but the student had no history whatsoever of criminal activity or of fraternizing with criminals.

The week-long search for him in the bayou came to nothing, despite the sonar divers, the helicopter and the K9's, and eventually, the case went cold; that was until 2013, when Matthew Mershon of KATV news announced; 'A possible break in the case.' It came when a letter was mysteriously sent to the Jacksonville Police Department.

The letter named individually a group of people allegedly involved in a missing persons case, and the letter writer believed these people could also be involved in Matthew's disappearance.

The original investigator Jim Kulesa and others of the

Lanoke P.D. joined forces with Jacksonville P. D. to investigate. A number of people were interviewed, including, says Kulesa 'an Elvis impersonator, but that didn't pan out,' and neither did any of the other people questioned. In fact, many of the people listed in the letter had already passed away. The police say they believe that evidence is still out there, but that the witnesses have not shown themselves.

Back during the original investigation, the lead investigator Frank Sturdivant was particularly determined to try to solve the case. Tragically, his own son had died of drowning. When Memphis magazine writer Marilyn Sadler went to his office, she could tell he'd followed every lead, no matter how small or irrelevant it might have seemed, desperate to find any clues.

He did wonder, had Matt drowned himself, in the bizarre pursuit of living as an Immortal Elf? But he also followed the work of the private investigator hired by the missing young man's parents.

This private investigator, who insisted on anonymity, found the aspects of his wet-up-to-the-knees jeans very curious and rather suspicions. "The drainage ditch between where his vehicle was found and where his clothes were laid was filled with water that would have come up much higher than his knees."

The private eye also discovered some very curious information, about an incident that occurred three weeks after the student had disappeared. He discovered that on December 28th, a trooper pulled over to check on a stationary Cadillac along the road close to where Matt had vanished from. The trooper found himself growing suspicious because he noticed that the man standing beside the Cadillac appeared to be trembling uncontrollably.

The trooper began to question the man and as he was doing so another man appeared, carrying a can of gasoline. The trooper thought perhaps the first man, who appeared to be the driver of the Cadillac, was shaking because he was cold (it was the middle of the winter) and he let them leave but noted down the license plate.

What the private eye discovered was that after this, later in the day, the Cadillac returned and the driver broke into a house on the same road, it would seem for the purpose of using the telephone in the house. When the owner of the house came home carrying groceries and opened the door, she screamed on seeing the intruder.

The intruder (the Cadillac driver) said calmly to the person they were speaking to on the woman's telephone, "I have to go. The lady of the house just came in."

Then he opened the front door and left, but as he did so, the lady whose house he had broken into noticed that in one of his hands he held a cell phone. Why then, she wondered, had he broken in to use her phone?

Once she was sure he had gone, the owner of the house went to her phone and pressed redial to see what number the intruder had called. When the person on the other end answered the phone, it turned out to be a convenience store located in North Little Rock, not far from the location of her house.

She handed the telephone number over to the private detective who ran a background check. He discovered that the worker who had answered the phone at the store had a criminal record.

The driver of the Cadillac was also background checked and in fact, only the next week after his home-invasion, he was arrested in Phoenix, Arizona for the possession of marijuana and mushrooms. The Cadillac itself was owned by someone else – a drug runner and counterfeiter who lived in Atlanta, very strangely only three miles from a friend of the missing student.

This friend had already been questioned by police, said the private eye, and he, as well as the police, had suspicions about him, he said. The private eye also emphasized how strange a coincidence it would be that in a large city like Atlanta, this friend and the drug dealer would live in such relatively close proximity.

The private eye told Memphis magazine that it went

further – there had been phone calls between the Cadillac driver and the friend of the missing student, on December 3rd. The private eye couldn't shake the chances that this was evidence of some kind of drug deal that had been planned and that the missing student had been talked into helping out with the deal, and as a result he had found himself there in the Bayou.

The private eye reasons that the student could have found himself way-in over his head or had a change of heart about participating and panicked – by which time everyone involved panicked and this tragically led to murder.

The private eye thinks the student's body could have been in the trunk of the Cadillac, and they'd brought his body back to bury it in the bayou somewhere, or that his body had been hid in the bayou and the Cadillac driver had returned to get it and bury it elsewhere. Memphis Magazine, following up on this to do their own fact checking however shed doubt on the private eye. The private eye was reticent and unwilling to reveal the telephone records for the supposed phone calls between the friend of the missing student and the Cadillac driver.

The private eye however said this was to protect his source. The original investigator, Detective Kulesa told the reporter however that he could find no records of such phone calls existing. The missing student's parents though were more inclined to believe the private eye, and called him tenacious and determined. Unfortunately, they too did not get any of the evidence in writing to confirm the Private eye's version of what may have happened.

Did the Cadillac driver have good reason to be shaking the day the trooper pulled over to talk to him, on the road so close to the Bayou? Or, was he simply cold? Was there any correlation to the Cadillac, the house break-in and the missing student? Or did Matt really think he wanted to wade into the water and become an immortal and live in another realm of reality with the Elven folk?

In 2013, original investigator Kulesa said, "Information we received is that this was a car-jacking." Does this mean it was entirely someone different to the uncontrollably shaking yet calm Cadillac-driver-turned-home-invader? And yet, at the end of it, no arrests have ever been made. Could this be another dead-end?

As the resolution for his parents remains sadly lacking, all that remains of Matthew are his abandoned clothing, that he either took off willingly, or unwillingly.... Eerily there was no sign of a struggle, no blood, no DNA and no way to track his scent.

Said Lt. James Kulesa, "It's probably one of the strangest mysteries I have ever come across since I've been in law enforcement."

His mother said, 'They found his scent from his clothes to the water's edge in the bayou, but the mystery is that there was no scent from his clothes to his car. And it's an absolute mystery to us and to the authorities to explain that. We have no clue what could have possibly happened.'

How could there possibly be no scent from his car to his clothes?

What possible way is there to even begin to explain this...?

Chapter Three

Missing Doctors, Missing Scouts

In June 2011, Dr. Michael Van Gortler and his daughter, 20-year-old Makana had gone to San Isabel National Forest in Colorado to hike. Dr. Michael was a 53-year-old E.R. physician and his daughter was studying medicine at the University of Colorado. They had gone to Missouri Mountain on a day of clear calm weather.

This was not their first hike, they had hiked together on many occasions. The father and daughter were last heard from on June 21, when Makana sent a text to her boyfriend telling him she was going hiking up the mountain with her father.

They were due back two days later. Her father was due to work in the emergency room in Boulder on the Sunday. By Tuesday, his ex-wife, Makana's mother, had called the Chaffee County Sheriff's Office to report them missing, after failing to get hold of her daughter. Rescuers launched a massive five-day air and ground search after finding their vehicle parked at the mountain's trailhead.

Their bodies were found 8 days later. Their bodies were found in steep terrain about 500 feet above the main trail, at an elevation of 12,000 feet, on the northeast side of Missouri Mountain within the forest, Chaffee County Sheriff W. Pete Palmer told Reuters. He said, "It's unclear how they died."

Sheriff Palmer said it had been one of the most extensive search and rescue operations the county had ever done. Over 200 rescuers searched the Mountain. The search lasted for five days and consisted of 18 search and rescue teams, along with dogs, the Sheriff's Office, the fire department, and two National Guard helicopters.

A military helicopter pilot dropping off a ground search and rescue team spotted what looked like two bodies. The coroner later reported; "They both died from blunt-force trauma to the head and neck." They had been found with catastrophic face and head injuries, at the bottom of a cliff.

Relatives told 7News they were "likely blown off a cliff." Coroner Mr. Amettis said the conditions of their bodies indicated that they had died on the day they set out on their hike and added that no crime had been committed. Their deaths were "an accident." He said their injuries were not inconsistent with falling.

Makana's aunt, Suzanne Katz, said Michael was a survivalist and always prepared with water, fire-building equipment and food every time he hiked. Describing him as "obsessive" when it came to preparing for their hikes, she said he always made an exhaustive list of what to pack, including collapsible containers for collecting rain water. He even once published an article on finding water sources in the backcountry.

The doctor had taken his daughter out on hikes ever since she was a child. Makana's cousin, Nicole Box, told 7NEWS that they were very experienced hikers and added that they were both very prepared for the climb. It was believed they had taken with them fire-starting equipment, water purifiers and dehydrated food.

Interestingly, Sheriff Palmer said; "It's a mystery that so many people take that trail and we hadn't had word of people seeing them."

The last person known to have seen them alive, at around 11.30 am on the 22nd, was hiker Jarrod Byrd. He said, "People are always up in the mountains having a good time and hiking. It was a nice day and I just thought they were going to be out for a nice hike. But, I think in the future I'm going to start warning people about being up on the mountain later in the day. You know, it just kind of goes to show, that anything can happen in the mountains..."

After being described as "Obsessive" when it came to preparing adequately for their hikes, to ensure their own health and safety, and having been hikers for so many years, doesn't it seem a bit odd that they both mysteriously "fell" off the cliff...?

We now come to another strange case involving a doctor. Trainee doctor Rachel Bagnall 25, and her boyfriend Jonathan Jette 34, an attaché for government in Quebec, both disappeared while hiking in rugged terrain.

The Vancouver residents vanished into thin air after they left for a two-day hike in the area around Cassiope and Saxifrage peaks, in the mountains north of Pemberton on September 4th, 2010.

The trail itself passes through some amazing forest. Two days after they were expected back, authorities found Jette's car parked on the Spetch Creek forest service road. A pair of sunglasses believed to be the trainee doctor's were found shortly after.

As five search and rescue crews were combing the back-country for the couple, a team located a pair of sunglasses believed to belong to Bagnall, but no other clues turned up. Jette's four door Toyota Echo contained his cell phone. Records showed that he made no calls after September 3rd.

An extensive air and ground search was conducted for the hikers, involving helicopters working three at a time. Numerous search and rescue and police teams also scoured the mountainous region, but there was no trace of them at all.

Repeated searches of the area they were believed to be in turned up no evidence at all about where they could be; no backpacks, no tents, nothing. Rachael was wearing a bright red-orange jacket.

A relative said the receipt for a newly-purchased axe was found in their vehicle but they were unsure exactly what other equipment the couple had with them.

Tim Lee, who was helping coordinate the search effort said, 'Our goal is we want to establish direction of travel.'

Jonathan Jette's father spent over a week in the Pemberton area continuing to try to find any clues he could about what happened to his son and his son's girlfriend. Bank statements revealed their last purchase was made on Jette's card at the diner 'Tim Hortons,' on the morning of September 4.

That was the last time any digital trace of them could be found. Police searched their homes, hacked into their Facebook accounts, checked cell phone records, searched their computers. No red flags were raised anywhere.

The families of the missing couple spent thousands upon thousands of dollars on private searches including hiring a group of highly-experienced mountain guides to survey the area in the hopes of finding evidence of their whereabouts.

It was believed they had sufficient water, food and other supplies to last for the 2-3 days they would be gone. RMCP sent a request out to anyone hiking in Cassiope-Saxifrage areas, through the Spetch Creek or Valentine Lake areas to be on the lookout for abandoned camping gear or clothing, and missing person's posters were circulated in the small towns of Squamish, Whistler, Pemberton, Mount Currie and D'Arcy.

The Lil'wat Nation assisted in the search. "They know the mountain inside and out," said relative Mike Jett. "They've gone on hikes themselves searching for clues and there are people that go berry picking and mushroom picking in the area around there. Those people are going to be our best chance of finding something," he said.

As spring came in 2013, two and a half years after their unexplained disappearance, Whistler-Pemberton RCMP spokesman Staff Sergeant Steve LeClair said they would be putting up new missing person's posters to remind hikers to keep an eye out for any signs of the couple's remains or belongings.

"We're hopeful we'll find the remains at some point," he said, "That might happen with people out hiking in the area." The previous fall, police had been searching the area again where their abandoned car had been found.

Jonathan Jette's mother, Lisa Grenier Jett, said, on unsolvedcanada.ca; "They were supposed to come back to Jonathan's apartment in Vancouver. Someone calls us the 9th of September to tell us that Jonathan and Rachael never came back from their hike. Sometimes I ask myself if something happened to them on the forest service road."

"The police, helicopters, SAR's, dogs, searched for them for ten days and they did not find anything - just Jonathan's car parked on that road. Volunteers continue and last summer we hired 3 pros who searched the ravines, the glaciers, and we did not find a clue. I ask myself many, many questions."

"We don't know what happened in this incident," said RMCP LeClair. "The fact that two people went missing is very unusual...."

At the spot where Rachel's sunglasses were found, it's almost as if the missing couple were 'snatched up' right there.

'Our goal is we want to establish direction of travel,' search organisers had said. Why was it so hard to find out which way they had gone...?

Now, yet another case involving a doctor, 63-year-old Jo Elliot-Blakeslee was a physician at the Snake River Correctional Institution in Ontario, Oregon. Her companion was 69-year-old retired teacher Amy Linkert from Idaho. They had met through their devoted work as missionaries.

In September 2013, they had gone to Craters of the Moon National Monument, in the Snake River Plain in Idaho. They were last seen on September 19th. They were reported missing on September 23rd, when co-workers of the doctor called police because she had not arrived for work that day as scheduled.

Officials believe the pair went only for a short hike at Craters, where their pickup was found, as their cell phones, purses and their dogs were still inside the vehicle.

On September 26th, Newspapers reported that one of the two women had been found dead. Butte County public information officer Tracy Weaver said 63-year-old Elliott-Blakeslee appeared to have died from exposure.

At first, Butte County deputies and park rangers believed they had found the Dr.'s body, but dental records confirmed it was in fact Linkert instead. Park Superintendent Dan Buckley said the Idaho National Guard and the Butte County Sheriff's search teams found the body by helicopter on a rugged part of the lava field.

The long-time Minneapolis special education teacher and missionary had purchased a Campervan as a retirement gift and had plans to take such trips as the one she was now missing from. "She was very happy and excited about going on this trip," her younger sister, Margaret Poirier said.

As searchers continued to comb the rocky terrain with a helicopter, dogs, and 70 volunteers looking for her companion, Parks spokeswoman Lori Iverson said Linkert had been dead for a few days when her body was found.

"Maybe Jo was injured, and they found a place for her to hunker down while Amy went for help and grew disoriented in the dark," said spokesman Iverson. "It's like an ocean of black lava rock and there are no landmarks."

More than 50 searchers, including eight dog teams and a crew of 21 firefighters, as well as two Blackhawk Helicopters continued the search for the other missing woman, focusing the search in a five-square mile area near Tree Molds, Broken Top Loop, and Wilderness trails on the south end of the monument.

"They left the trail for some reason and a tragedy occurred," Linkert's sister said. "My heart goes out to Jo's family. Our family is concerned and distressed they can't find her."

Unfortunately, the search for her was partly carried out during a Government shutdown, although Ted Stout, a spokesman for the Park, said three of them were still working, searching for the missing women. Park officials had asked for and been given a waiver to enable them to keep 10 trained rangers on hand for the on-going search, along with the three-person skeleton crew, although none knew if they would get paid. Caving experts also joined the search, expanding the search to the hundreds of caves in the area.

On October 23rd, newspapers reported; 'Search crews have finally found the body of Idaho hiker Dr. Elliott-Blakeslee. Rescue workers aboard a helicopter found Elliot-Blakeslee's body about a mile from where they found the body of her hiking partner.

Why did it take them so long to find her body, when it was in the exact area they had been searching for a month?

How did these terrible deaths happen? They must have surely only been intending to go for a short walk, because they had made the decision to leave their cell phones in the car, their belongings, and most importantly their dogs in the car. They clearly had not intended to be away from their car for long. How did they become separated by a mile between them?

Interestingly, the doctor had been an officer in the Naval Reserves, retiring with the rank of Commander in the 1990's. Their families said they were convinced the pair wouldn't have headed off the trail, because their dogs were in the vehicle.

Isn't it odd that it took so long to find the second woman? - When the search focussed on a small radius, encompassing 6,000 volunteer search hours.

"They were both avid hikers and survivalists, said Tammy Kerklow, Amy's niece. "This is very strange."

Why did it take them so long to find the second body....?

~~~

A frantic four-day search was conducted for missing boy scout Brennan Hawkins in June 2005. 3,000 volunteers had been involved in the hunt for 11-year-old Brennan.

He disappeared when he became separated from his scout group while in the High Uintas, about 60 miles east of Salt Lake City at the Bear River Boy Scout Reservation. He had last been seen at approximately 5.30 pm near a climbing wall.

He had been struggling to get his safety harness off. Fox news reported 'Officials said Brennan disappeared somewhere along a dirt road between the camp's artificial climbing wall and the food hall, where he was going to meet his friend but never showed up.'

"We had searchlights and helicopters and thousands of people," said Chief Deputy for the Summit County Sherriff's office, David Booth.

Deputies feared that although predators lurked in the area; bears cougars and wolves, the biggest risk was that he had fallen into the cold fast-flowing river. They were also cognisant of the fact that the year before, a 12-year-old boy called Garrett Bardsley had vanished while camping at a nearby lake. He has never been found.

At another nearby lake, a mother and daughter had disappeared in 2003. Their bodies had been found nine months later.

'What happened in the woods,' asked People Magazine, of the strange disappearance of the boy scout.

Said his mother, "I held my cell phone the entire drive," when she learnt he had vanished. "I'm thinking; they're going to call any minute and say they found him. I mean how can you lose a child with 1,400 people around?"

Among the searchers was Kevin Bardsley, whose own son 12-year-old son Garrett, had vanished the year before while they were camping there.

By 6 a.m. the morning after Brennan vanished, the area was literally teeming with search and rescue teams. By the third day, he still hadn't been found.

"They still haven't come up with anything," said his mother. Deep-water rescue teams had searched the river, which was only 100 yards from the road the boy was believed to have been walking on after he got separated from his friends.

Rescuers had found three socks and a shoe in the river, but they didn't belong to the little boy and there was no sign of him. Then, just when his family and all the searchers had about lost all hope, he was found. A 43-year-old painter from Salt Lake City, Forrest Nunley, had joined the hunt for the little boy. He found Brennan, "standing in the middle of the trail."

Said his mother, "People say that the heavens are closed, and God no longer answers prayers. We are here to tell you – the heavens are not closed! Prayers are answered, and children come home."

"He was all muddy and wet," said painter Nunley when he saw him. The little boy appeared to be physically ok although a little delirious. He asked for some water. He'd survived for four days without food water or shelter.

He told his mother that at night, "He tucked his legs under his sweatshirt and curled up next to a tree. He drank water from the creeks." He told his rescuer that he had seen some searchers on horseback but that he had been scared in case they were bad guys, and he hid from them when he spotted them.

Nunley said Brennan just happened to walk out on the road right where he was. He was five miles from the scout camp. "He was just standing there in the middle of the trail!"

Sheriff Dave Edmunds said he thought the little boy had walked up a ridge for several miles from the point where he went missing. Curiously, early reports had said he had crossed a river and was wet when found, as Nunley the painter reported too, but later newspaper reports stated he had not crossed a river and was not wet.

Scout leader Martin Christensen says he thinks he know the route Brennan must have taken after he got lost. He thinks the little boy took a wrong turn from the climbing wall walking toward his tent instead of the food hall. Then, when he realized he had gone the wrong way, he doubled back through some burned woods but then took another wrong turn at the first trail he came to.

What really surprised the searchers though was that he followed the steep trail out of a narrow river valley, where, said Newspapers, 'The scout camp was hard to miss and then continued on, climbing 400 feet over a mountain range and went farther away.'

"He went way uphill," said Scout leader Christensen. "Ninety per cent of kids who get lost will go downhill – he went uphill." His journey took him about five miles on foot.

His parents said they did not intend on pushing for answers from their son about his time alone in the woods and did not want to be questioned further, reported Deseret News.

Brendan's mother had said, "When we brought him home, his voice was different. He said he was hoarse from shouting for help. He saw a helicopter one day and yelled to be noticed."

Why could nobody see him? Helicopters and 3,000 volunteers were all searching.

For Kevin Bardsley, who had joined the search parties to help look for Brennan, there must have been mixed emotions when he was found, because his own son, 12-year-old Garrett, had vanished the year before while they were camping there, and has never been found.

'Loss of Boy Scout is called Unexplainable,' Associated Press reported a year earlier, in 2004. 12-year-old Bardsley Garrett had gone camping and fishing with his father and scout group on August 20th, 2004, when he disappeared from Cuberant Lake in the Uinta Mountains.

As the father and son were sitting together beside the lake fishing, at an elevation of 10,200 feet, the boy got his shoes and pants wet and his father told him to go back to their camp and fetch dry socks and pants. It was around 8 am when this happened.

His father watched as the boy walked off on the trail and into the trees. He could never have imagined that would be the last time he would see his son.

The campsite he was heading to was about a quarter of a mile from the lake and it was a well-established path that connected with a road another quarter of a mile away. According to a family friend, the distance from where they were fishing to the camp was "No more than 150 paces."

The father and son were with a scout group of 7 adults and 18 boys, on a scout's trip. More than 200 volunteers gathered to help the search and rescue teams search into the night for the boy after he failed to return to camp or to his father fishing. He had no provisions with him when he vanished. Searchers looked for him on foot and horseback for days in the mountainous terrain.

The only clue they ever found was one of his socks. They found his sock in a boulder field above the lake, about half a mile from where he had sat fishing with his dad.

"The sock appears that it was taken off a wet foot, and wadded up," said Summit County Sherriff Dave

Edmunds, "Consistent with what we know about Garrett."

The Sheriff said searchers would now be concentrating their efforts on searching the boulder field and close-by surroundings for the boy, who they presumed would be found dead.

The bowhunting season had started and hunters were told to be on the look-out for a boy. The Sheriff's office put up missing person's posters near the trailheads and handed them out to campers and hikers and hunters.

"We're never going to stop looking," Sheriff Edmunds said, but they must have stopped, and certainly, no trace of the boy was ever found.

His father, Kevin Bardsley explained that the last time he saw his boy, he had shouted directions to him as he watched him walk off back to camp. His son had almost taken the wrong path but on hearing his father shout to him, he got onto the right path that led into the woods.

How or why he ended up in a boulder field is, as newspapers reported 'Unexplainable,' and from one searcher who happened to be camping in the same area at the time, there is another query. 'Sound carries up there in the basin,' they say, as they tested this when there.

If that's the case, why could the boy not hear any of the searchers shouting his name...?

This searcher says; "I was camped at Cuberant when he went missing and spent the day helping to look for him. His group was actually camped in the meadow just up from Cuberant. This is the meadow you pass by just after going over the pass and dropping down into the Cuberant basin. He and his father Kevin had been fishing at Cuberant that morning. Up at Cuberant we could hear members of his group yelling his name that morning he went missing. The sound carries up there in the basin.

That night we spent up there after he disappeared was one of the most awful nights of my life, knowing that poor kid was out there in the cold while I was safe and warm in my sleeping bag. I went back up the next week to spend another day searching. It bothers me to this day...'

Chapter Four

Missing Children, Missing Rangers

A Ranger disappears....

22-year-old David Barclay Miller had been working as a seasonal employee of the forest service for two months. He was an experienced outdoorsman.

He was last seen by co-workers on May 19th, 1998, at the Beaver Creek Ranger Station leaving with a green backpack for a two-and-a-half-day hike in Sedona. He was said to be an experienced hiker who had climbed Mount Rainer and explored much wilderness in Alaska before moving to Sedona.

His vehicle was found abandoned at the Vultee Arch Trail. He had signed in at the Trailhead. This trail is designated as 'easy' and is a fairly short and popular trail so it could be assumed he was hiking further, but he never returned.

A huge search was launched after he failed to return, with his co-workers searching for him along with the Sheriff's Office and Search and Rescue parties with dogs, but no trace of him was ever found.

Sheriff's spokesman Curt Milam said searchers had done all they could to find David. They mystery remains as to what happened to him, because he was never found.

In a different case, 'an autopsy Monday revealed that a 12-year old boy who fell into a crevasse in Rocky Mountain National Park died of massive skull fractures," reported Associated Press, in 1982.

'The body of 12-year-old Robert Baldeshwiler was discovered by a trio of climbers on a steep slope about 800 feet above Emerald Lake. The climbers had been alerted to the missing boy by signs posted at trail heads.'

Robert Baldeschwiler disappeared, on June 29, 1982, 'when he vanished during a hike in the area with his parents. A $130,000 search failed to reveal any trace of the boy. The search was suspended July 5.'

'The boy had run ahead of his family to climb Flattop Mountain alone. He was last seen by a hiker descending the mountain trail.'

'The boy's body was found in an area that had been searched several times. At the height of the six-day search 220 people, five dogs and a Chinook were involved in one of the most expensive rescue efforts in park history.'

Is it strange that they did not find him in all the previous searches?

In another odd case, 'Body of Missing Boy Found Beside Creek Near His House,' reported Associated Press on March 1st, 1999.

In April 1999, in Norton, Massachusetts, 9-year-old

Corey Anderson disappeared while out searching for his dog after it ran off. He was 'found dead four days later,' according to news reports, 'near a shallow stream about 300 yards from his family's home, in an area that had been searched several times before.'

'The body of Corey Anderson was found curled in a ball in dense underbrush along the banks of an icy brook after the stripes of his Boston Bruins jacket caught a searcher's eye,' police said. Unsure about how he had died, police said they did not think he drowned.

Associated Press asked, 'Why the boy would be in such a spot - with growth so thick that an adult would have to crawl on hands and knees to enter?'

They said, 'Search crews in canoes found his body, on the bank of Mulberry Brook.' Strangely, 'It was the fifth time that the area had been searched.'

The young boy's disappearance occurred during a fierce snowstorm and at the time it received national attention, as hundreds of searchers voluntarily combed every inch of the neighbourhood looking for him. The five searches for him involved boats, horses, dogs and hundreds of search and rescue personnel, state police, firefighters and local citizens. The boats searched the lake and the swamps behind his house and a helicopter hovered over the woods and bogs.

At the time of his disappearance, the little boy was wearing a sweater, two jackets, and fur-lined boots. A snow storm had come in and lain up to 7 inches of snow on the ground. The family's dog had run out of the house on the day he went missing, and the boy had gone in search of his beloved pet. Sadly, though the dog was found in a neighbour's yard shortly after, the little boy did not make it back home. He was missing for four days.

CNN reported, 'The search for a missing 9- year-old boy came to a grim end when a search party found him dead Sunday.' Police trooper Paul Hartley told reporters, 'He was curled in a ball. His body was found on swampy land about 15 feet from a shallow stream.'

When asked if foul play was suspected, Lt. Paul Maloney said, "To the best of my knowledge, no, but as a matter of procedure, this is the process we have to follow to eliminate that possibility." Lt. Leo Gerstel, with the state police underwater recovery team, was among those who found the youngster's body. He wouldn't speculate on the cause of death.' "I don't think he drowned. He didn't appear to be wet but beyond that I wouldn't venture how he expired."

Police trooper Hartley said he didn't think they were going to find him where they did, in dense underbrush. "I thought that the terrain was impenetrable for a boy that age, and I was just shocked that he was actually there, because I never thought a boy in a blizzard could go that distance."

CNN pointed out that his body had been found by a 'search party in a canoe in an area searched four previous times.'

Perhaps this was because snow had covered the boy, and yet 'Police aren't sure what brought Corey to the nearly impenetrable marsh. Nor do they know how the boy made his way amid brambles and brush so dense that an adult would have to crawl on hands and knees to reach the site.'

'Searchers had visited the site repeatedly,' in a 'round-the-clock search for Corey. Crews used horses, canoes, professional divers, snowmobiles and dogs in their quest for the boy. A National Guard helicopter equipped with an infrared tracking device flew over the area.'

The police think the simplest answer is that he got lost, and perhaps it is as simple as that, even though he was reported as being found "in an area searched four previous times," but what it doesn't do is explain how he managed to get into an area described as 'nearly impenetrable marsh...amid brambles and brush so dense,' and it does call to mind the strange case of Todd Sees.

In 2002, the strange story of what happened to Todd Sees began to circulate. Just after 5am on August 4th, Todd left his rural home in Northumberland,

Pennsylvania to go up into the nearby mountain to do some pre-season deer scouting. As he left home, he told his family he would be home by midday.

When he didn't return his concerned wife alerted authorities, knowing it was completely out of character for him not to return as he'd said he would. By 2pm, a search party had been organized. The State police and a couple hundred local volunteers began to search for him. Quickly they discovered his four-wheeler at the top of the mountain, but search dogs could find no scent to go on.

The search carried on for two days, from top to bottom of the mountainous area.

On the second day a break came; something was seen in a thick brush area beside a pond, very close to the family home. The search party spent half an hour hacking at the brush to get to it. What they found was Todd Sees' body, virtually naked. He was wearing just his underwear. When he'd left two days before, he'd been fully dressed in outdoor clothing and boots.

His body was not bloated; it was emaciated. Immediately there were concerns. That would not be the usual condition to find a body in.

It got stranger. Though many locals claimed afterward there was nothing unusual about the incident, others, including Emmy award winning investigative journalist Linda Molten Howe, and Peter Davenport of the National UFO Reporting Centre, believed there was a lot more to the case. They pointed to the fact that the area had been previously searched, and yet the tracker dogs had not been able to pick up his scent at all. Why?

This led to speculation that his body could not have been there when the area was searched but was perhaps placed there later. His body was found in a thickly forested spot, so difficult to access that it led many to believe he could not have gone there voluntarily, by his own volition, if the searchers themselves had to hack their way into it to retrieve him.

But who or what had taken him in there if it was such a difficult area to get to?

Even odder, one of his missing boots was later found; high up in a tree a mile from where his vehicle was found, and no-where near his body. People wanted to know how the boot could have got up there.

There were claims that upon the discovery of his body, the FBI arrived, cordoning off the area and refusing to allow the family access to Todd. It's implied by researchers including ex-detective Butch Witkowski, that Sees was an unfortunate victim of an alien abduction. Their claims are allegedly back up by reports of sightings by three local farmers of a large bright object just above the power lines, hovering in the area at the time of Sees disappearance.

The official cause of his death was ruled as a cocaine overdose. Those close to him were reported as stating that he was not a drug taker. The case however is entirely strange in that some reports say the man never even existed! Point Township police chief Gary Steffen said the case is an 'open investigation' and there were no apparent signs of foul play, according to Peter Davenport of National UFO Reporting Canter.

On the other hand, due to lack of available official records about Todd and his case, others think it could even be a wild hoax....

~~~~

A tragic case now involves little Stephen McCarron, aged five years, who had been very much looking forward to spending a week with his aunt and uncle at their home in Ayr, on the west coast of Ayrshire in Scotland. He was particularly looking forward to visiting the 'Wonderwest World Holiday Park,' a seaside amusement park with fair-ground rides and games. Formerly known as 'Butlin's,' it was part of a very popular chain of holiday parks.

Sadly, his happy experience there on September 17th 1988, would turn into the largest ever missing child hunt by Scottish Police, with more than 200 police officers searching the camp and the countryside surrounding the camp.

All went well at first, when Stephen arrived at the Park with his aunt Lyn, and uncle Ian Sneddon. He spent the first half an hour enjoying various rides and amusements among all the other children and parents. Then, as his aunt and uncle, who had stood watching him, suddenly realized they could no longer see him, panic set in. Of course, they began to search the ride, search the crowds leaving and queuing for the ride, searched all around now, shouting his name ever more frantically until they gave up – they could see him nowhere.

They ran from ride to ride searching for him but found no sign of him anywhere. They searched everywhere inside the amusement park until they realized it was time to alert the park employees, who were quick to call the police. Soon, 200 hundred police would become involved in the search for the missing little boy.

A Royal Navy helicopter made a preliminary search covering a two-mile radius. The ground search extended to a 6-mile radius around the amusement park, and it sparked one of the largest searches ever seen in Scotland.

Gerry Gallacher was part of the team tasked with

finding the little boy and has since spoken of the torment he felt ever since it happened; "Search parameters were established by senior management and assistance was eventually sought from the RAF, which provided a helicopter equipped with infrared sensors." Gallacher was one of the detectives drafted in to assist by interviewing staff and guests at the holiday park that day.

Meanwhile, divers were brought in to search the local rivers and waterways. A heat-seeking helicopter was brought in – but not for two days. Coastguards and holiday centre staff had by then searched the near-by beaches.

'The surrounding area was bleak, cold and marshy and he was only a child, woefully underdressed for the conditions and night-time temperatures,' said Gallacher to Scotland's Daily Star Newspaper.

The police search was heavily criticised when little Stephen was found dead, 16 days later. 'I'm sure most of the inquiry team were satisfied that Stephen was missing and not the victim of foul play, but that didn't make things any easier,' said Gallacher.

'Although there were initial concerns that Stephen may have been abducted, they were offset by a witness who saw a boy fitting his description and wearing the same clothes climbing a six-foot perimeter fence.'

One witness, an employee of the Park, claimed to have seen the little boy in a distressed state in one of the Café's at the amusement park. Barmaid Jacqueline Hepburn said she had seen a man and a boy, who was crying. She said she heard the man say: "Don't worry. Your mother would not have gone and left you. I am going to look after you."

She said the man lifted the child up and as he did, so the child began hitting him and screaming. She said the middle-aged man "wore a snorkel-type jacket. The boy was crying as the man carried him off." Another witness however said she was sure that Stephen was alone when he left the amusement park.

A witness said she saw a boy fitting his description, wearing the same clothes as Stephen was wearing, climbing a six-foot perimeter fence.

Grandmother, Mrs Margaret Park, was with her family in a caravan beside the perimeter fence of the complex when she saw a youngster walking past. She said he stopped and looked directly in at her inside the caravan. She said that she sent her grandson to find out what the boy was doing, and her grandson told her the boy had climbed out of the complex over the fence.

He showed her where the little boy had climbed, and she could see a sag in the fence there. She said her grandson had spoken to the young boy - who she identified as Stephen - as he sat on top of the fence and asked if he was lost. The boy had said 'No.'

Later, after his death, three people told the fatal accident inquiry they had seen him in the company of a man. Local businessman Mr. Stuart Reid told of seeing Stephen walking along the road hand-in-hand with a man. "It struck me as kind of strange," he told the inquiry, as it was a cold night and the man was warmly dressed but the child wore only a T-shirt.

A Mr. Bryan Wilcox told the inquiry he had met a man with a young boy as he drove over the single-track road which cuts across the Carrick hills where Stephen's body was eventually found. He said it was close to darkness and they were walking side-by-side, holding hands. "They looked as if they were out for a walk." Of course, these sightings were made when not everyone was aware the little boy had disappeared. Although the search was publicised, it's likely that not everyone in the area had heard about it, or they surely would have intervened if even slightly suspicious?

Contrasting these testimonies, during the search for the missing boy, a number of motorists believed that they had spotted the little boy walking alone along the road. At the time he went missing, Police had of course wondered if he had been abducted, but yet there were many witnesses who said they thought they had seen the little boy walking along the road away from the Amusement park, alone. Why did none of them stop to ask if this 5-year-old, walking alone, was alright? There were further sightings of a little boy walking alone on a road towards nearby Ayr. The ongoing police investigation at the time however, had ruled out foul play quite early, according to Gallacher.

Lady MacLehose, 68, of Maybole, found Stephen's body in a ditch 16 days later while out walking with her dog, on Sunday October 2nd, 6 miles away from the amusement park. She went home and called the police.

His body was lying just outside the search parameters. It was determined that he had died of exposure. He was found curled up in a ditch, most probably in that position in an attempt to keep warm.

Inspector Redmond said that when the little boy was found, the shoes he was wearing were tied with double knots and there was a muddy sock in the boy's trouser pockets. His father did not think his son was capable of tying his own laces, but the Chief Inspector said he read nothing sinister into that. The evidence suggested to the Chief Inspector that the boy had got into mud, taken his socks off, then slipped his tied shoes back on.

He said that there had been no apparent effort to conceal the body in the ditch where it was found. 'There were about 1000 places in the immediate area where a body could have been concealed and probably never found.' It was a remote, isolated landscape of fields and ditches.

Initially, a Navy helicopter had made a preliminary search covering a two-mile radius around the holiday centre. This same area was later painstakingly cross-checked, yet they did not see the missing boy during these searches.

Experts had told the Police Inspector in charge of organising the search for Stephen that "there was a 92% probability that the child would be found within 2.2 miles." The child's body was found in a ditch 4.6 miles as the crow flies, 6 miles in all reality from the holiday complex.

'The surrounding area was bleak, cold and marshy and

he was only a child, woefully underdressed for the conditions and night-time temperatures,' Detective Gallacher said.

So how did he manage to walk all that way, across marches? Quite how he got 6 miles away across the fields and boggy marshes, has never been determined. It was a desolate place.

Chapter Five

More Vanishing Children

In 1932 on the Island of Leka, in the coastal region of Trondelag, Norway, 3-year-old Svanhild Hartvigsen disappeared. Her story would become legendary in Norway.

On Sunday June 5th, 1932, the little girl had gone with her family to Church to attend the Christening of her little brother. After the service, the family, along with other relatives went to a nearby farm for refreshments.

At approximately 3.30pm, Svanhild was out playing with the other children. She was in a field beside the farmhouse, while the older children had decided to take off and head to the sea shore. At some point it was suddenly realized that she had vanished.

Within 10 minutes, a full comprehensive and organized

search for her began. Since there were many relatives and friends at the farm already, there was a good-sized group available to set out on a search for her. There were an estimated 200 searchers. None expected to look very far before finding her; she had been playing within view of them only moments earlier.

The search party included the entire male choir who had attended her little brother's christening, but by dark that evening they had still not found her. They did however find her handkerchief, and then one of her shoes – on the mountainside.

On finding her abandoned shoe, several of the search party decided to scale the mountain to investigate. The younger members of the search party, including Karl Haug, Leif Anderson, and Jentoft Sevendsen began the steep incline, although it took them an hour or more to walk over the sharp stones that lined the path to the mountain.

In a later interview they said; "We were not prepared at all. We still had our Church clothes on." When they got close to the top of the mountain, one stood on the other's shoulders to reach the summit where a narrow rock shelf was hanging below the peak. There, the searcher was stunned to see the little girl hiding in a small cave at the back of the ledge.

He managed to reach her and persuaded her to come out from her hiding-hole, although she appeared terrified. He successfully brought her back down the mountain. He carried her back down to his friends and from there they hurriedly escorted her back to her parents.

Other than a scratch on her forehead, she appeared physically well, although her clothes were ripped in places, particularly across her chest. Her foot, which was shoeless, appeared unmarked and uninjured. She had been missing for 7 hours.

How did she get to the top of a mountain ledge? One of her rescuers, Karl Haug, had returned with his shoes completely torn up from walking over the rough stones at the base of the mountain, it was that inhospitable.

Yet the shoe remaining on Savnhild's foot was still intact and not dirty, nor was the sock she wore on her other foot.

The local Doctor, Dr. K. Fossum found no serious injuries on her body, and other than being in a terrible state of shock, she appeared no worse for wear.

Speculation grew that the only possible way she could have got to that mountain ledge, 250 metres up and 2 kilometres from her play area, had to have been in the mouth of an eagle. An eagle must have abducted her and flown her there. In fact, this is what the little girl went on to tell her parents had happened.

She told them that a great big bird had swooped down on her as she was playing in the field. She said it had caught hold of her in its mouth and flown away with her. The rips in her clothing were presumed to have been caused by the eagle's claws.

Although now deceased, Svanhild stuck to her account about what happened to her that day, and she expressed concern that many people were sceptical of what she said had occurred. "I was playing with some stones when suddenly I saw the eagle coming towards me. The next thing I remember is lying on a ledge and then I see the eagle dive toward me."

"I remember how it came at me with those big claws. Horrible! I was only three, but I had an instinct to fight, to survive. It would probably have torn me to pieces and carried me up to the nest to feed its kids. I remember what I experienced," she said vehemently, although she always said she could not remember actually flying with the eagle as a child, nor when she grew up. She did remember throwing stones at the eagle once it landed on the ledge on the mountain and deposited her there.

As she lay helplessly, she scrabbled around with her hands for any stones on the ledge to try to defend herself with as the eagle began to savagely try to peck at her. It is possible that she could not remember flying with the eagle because of the shock it caused her. She may even have perhaps fainted from shock, but those who are sceptical of her account say she would surely have remembered that part.

Yet, if an eagle had not flown her up to the ledge, how else could she have possibly got there, with 1 shoe and clean socks?

In a retrospective account, Norway's Dagbladet magazine writes, 'Over her, the silent shadow glides by a tall eagle. Soon the bird will tear the girl up from the hot summer field, fly two hundred yards to the sky and place the nearly twenty kilos heavy Svanhild on an inaccessible mountain shelf in Hagafjellet.'

'While the eagles scream for food, the girl must throw pebbles to keep the big bird away. She does not see the abyss beneath her eyes, for her eyes cover her hands to protect herself from the sharp beak every time the eagle stumps against her."

When she was in her eighties, she said: "I suddenly saw the eagle coming towards me. The next thing I remember is that I'm lying on a mountain shelf and then I see the eagle plunge down at me. It was a cruel experience. The dress I had was torn. I just have to be thankful. Over the years I have heard many stories about children and animals that have been taken by eagles. But I am probably the only one who has come out of it with my life and for that I am grateful."

At the time of her abduction, she weighed around 12 kg. Ornithologist Alv Ottar Folkestad, head of the Norwegian Ornithological Society, and with much experience in both practical and theoretical calculations on the weight large eagles can carry, said, "My experience is that the eagle has a well-developed ability to perceive size and weight. I have been researching eagles of all weights and classes and sea trout for thirty years, and I have never seen an eagle lift anything heavier than 3.2 kg. She was too heavy."

The abducted girl had indeed weighed significantly more than that. "I do not want to blame anyone for lying, but no one can abolish the laws of physics! In my eyes, there is no doubt: this has never happened."

Author Bente Roestad, who published the book Ørnerovet in Leka in 2006 said about the saga, presumably tongue in cheek, that even extremely unlikely events may occur: "The Hagafjället is a special mountain, the wind conditions this day were special, and it has been a unique eagle: a Muhammad Ali among the eagles!" In other words, she too finds the explanation that a bird took her, unlikely.

Yet the reason the three searchers, Haug, Sevndson and Anderson had gone up the mountain was that people in the area had said they thought there was an eagle's nest up there. The skeptics asked however, how could the young girl have no eagle feathers on her at all? And they asked, how reliable was the testimony of the three young men who had found her? Had they really found her in the circumstances they described? Yet there was nothing to suggest these three men, all members of the Church choir, were not honest upstanding citizens either.

She had managed to get to an area inaccessible enough that for an adult to reach it, they had to stand on the shoulders of another adult to reach the ledge, and the journey to reach the base of the mountain before they climbed it had destroyed one man's pair of shoes, it was that rough to cross. Yet she had lost a shoe but her foot was uninjured and clean.

Those who believe in her version say that it is impossible for a 3-year-old child to walk that far and climb that high, in one shoe and with a perfectly clean foot.

How did she get there if it wasn't in the mouth of an eagle?

Reports from as far back as the 1800's talk of giant birds kidnapping children and flying them away to their deaths. In 1838, a 5-year-old child called Marie Delex was out playing with a friend on the alpine mountainside of Valais, Switzerland.

All of a sudden, a huge eagle appeared and came down, swooping at them. It caught hold of the little girl and flew off with her in its beak.

A huge search party was launched to find the missing child, and in time, a giant eagle's nest was discovered. Inside the nest were two baby eagles nestled among the remains of sheep and goats' bodies. But there was no sign of the little girl.

It was not until eight weeks later that a shepherd came across her mutilated body as it lay on a rock, one and a half kilometres from where she had been snatched.

In another account, according to fortean researchers Bob Rickard and John Mitchel, in 1950 'high on a desolate crag above Saint-Maurice in the French Alps, a Swiss mountain guide found a child's skeleton.' The remains were identified as those of a four-year-old boy who had vanished from the nearby village 3 years before.'

'There was no way the child could have climbed there, so it was widely agreed that he must have been carried to the ledge by a giant eagle.'

Chapter Six

Missing Hunters

On October 15th, 2013, 74-year-old Barry Zeldin left his home in Mays Landing, in Hamilton New Jersey. He told his wife he was planning to go and put bait at a deer stand near Chatsworth in the Warren Grove Recreation Area.

As was standard practise, he signed in at the Audubon Gun Club just before 10 a.m. "They always sign in," said his wife Janet, "so the hunters know who is out there."

When her husband failed to return home that night and did not call his wife of 50 years, she was not alarmed. He was, she said, "very independent," and he would often go on hunting trips that could last several days. "I figured he got a deer and he was looking for it. I didn't think much of it."

By Tuesday however, she began to phone him every hour, but she got no answer. On Wednesday she continued to repeatedly try to get hold of him on his cell phone. All she kept getting was his voicemail.

On Thursday, she got into her car and headed for the Gun Club. Unfortunately, she could not locate the club on her own and returned home.

The following day she tried again, and this time she did find the Gun Club and she quickly explained her circumstances. Several of the members immediately volunteered to go with her to look for her husband.

Wilbur Swales, president of the Gun Club told CBS local news, 'We went out Friday night looking for him and we couldn't find nothing. We went out Saturday, and we found his automobile." It was parked on FAA Tower Road.

His Blazer SUV was unlocked, his cell phone was on the dashboard, his keys were still in the ignition and his dog was sitting inside. The dog had managed to survive by drinking rain water as it fell on the car (the car windows had been left open) and by eating the bait that had been intended for the deer.

State Park Police and the New Jersey State Police began a search for him. They searched the heavily wooded area all weekend, bringing in the helicopter and K-9's. As Sunday afternoon came and no sign of him was found, the official search was called off.

His wife was not frantic at this point. She'd known him as a hunter for 50 years. She said, "I know he's good in the woods; that's why I never worried. He knows what he's doing in the woods; he's an avid hunter, he could probably survive out here indefinitely."

She knew him well enough – they'd been married for a quarter of a century and they'd owned a Café for many years.

Volunteers with Burlington County K-9 Search and Rescue arrived on the following Tuesday to search the woods. Where he had gone missing was very dense woodland. The Warren Grove Recreation Area encompasses the central region of the Pine Barrens.

Access to the spot at which he had parked up and gone to the deer stand is not on an established trail. Access to the Grove is via narrow sand roads. The weather during this time was moderate with temperatures in the 60's Fahrenheit but with a wind chill factor.

With the official search called off now, on October 19th his daughter-in-law Debbie said, "We refuse to stand by and do nothing when the NJSP aren't out there searching! The family and friends have been searching the woods every day."

Coming from Kentucky to help look for her father-in-law, she was appealing for volunteers to help her on NJPB, a forum for the New Jersey Pine Barrens.

One forum member replied; 'It seems that a hunter should be easy to find in that spot. The area is densely vegetated, and signs of foot traffic should be noticeable. Hunters don't deviate far from established paths and habits I would think. I'm very surprised he hast been found.'

Another member said, 'They marked off the trees with streamers which extended all the way back to the cedar swamps,' noting that the search for the missing man appeared to have been "extensive."

Another of the group said, "I believe the area has been searched quite well, however it's very dense. We never saw any evidence of birds or anything either, so I'm just not sure he's there. Might have been taken elsewhere yet foul play doesn't make sense as his belongings were left in his truck."

"He doesn't seem to be the type to walk away on his own; I would think he would have taken his dog. The dog being left in the car along with wallet & cell makes me feel he stopped to check his tree stands & didn't plan to be gone long."

For an indication of just how dense it is there, this is a good description; "His truck was found right by the path to his stand. We had to fight our way through this stuff like nobody knows. Cedars so close together that you could not swing your arms in a circle even with your elbows bent."

Was he lying hidden there? And yet, what would have made him fall into a thicket so dense that it cocooned him, imprisoning him?

Besides which, the dogs had failed to find his scent – surely, they would have led searchers to the spot he was lying trapped in?

Guy Thompson uploaded a photograph to the forum. It was a pair of coveralls. He said, "We did find these very deep in the woods. Found them on a survey cut which might mean it was one of the surveyors who owned them."

"There always is a chance that even though he had shorts on, he could have had overalls in his truck and put them on to walk in the woods. They may be his."
He photographed the coveralls but left them where he

found them. On their way out of the woods they encountered what seemed to be searchers on a practice search. He told the volunteer search organization what he'd just come across out there, but he said they weren't interested and insisted the missing man had shorts on.

Several of the missing reports however say the missing man was wearing jeans and a flannel shirt.

On November 7th, three weeks after Zedlin disappeared, his wife told reporters, "There've been different rescuers, state troopers, neighbours, friends and the fire department. In two weeks, the shotgun hunters will be going out, and there should be about 1,000 of them pushing for deer... I don't want to speculate about what could have happened." She was hoping her husband would still be found alive.

'People that are lost and frightened often do crazy stuff like strip and run naked till collapsing. Fear probably makes 'em feel stifled and running will overheat them.'
'They'll even run across a blacktop road and straight

into the woods on the other side not realizing they've crossed a road. I've talked to trackers who have seen this sort of thing,' said one experienced hunter.

If this had been the case for the missing hunter, what could have made him flee in a desperate panic, removing his clothing as he fled?

Or, perhaps they simply belonged to someone else, although either way, hunters or workers wouldn't usually leave their protective clothing behind, would they?

Sadly, he has never been found.

Another very unsettling case of a man who went into the woods and never came back, happened when he was working as part of a four-man survey crew. It took place in Harris County, Georgia. It was January 25th, 2002 when 20-year-old

Christopher Carlton Thompkins said 'Goodbye' to his mum and left the home he shared with her to drive to work. What his mother could never have imagined was that this would be the last time she would ever see her son.

"I need closure," she told the Ledger Enquirer, after six years had passed with no sign of her son. "I need to know what happened that day, and where my son's body is."

Her son was last seen in a wooded area between Warm Springs Road and Georgia 85 near County Line Road. His mother relates what she knows:

"He left home about 8:10 a.m. He parked his car at work and drove to the job-site with the surveyor he worked for. At the time, I was also employed by the surveyor's family as their baby-sitter. He worked that morning with three other employees in a lightly wooded area off County Line Road. All the workers were about 50 feet from each other, walking in the same direction."

"Around 1 p.m. the surveyor phoned his wife to inform her that Christopher was missing. One of Christopher's co-workers said Christopher was walking in the same direction as the others. When he looked away and then looked back, Chris was gone."

His mother didn't immediately know her son had mysteriously vanished. "I was not informed until 4:15 p.m." She adds that she was not allowed to file a missing person's report until 24 hours had passed.

In the meantime, she says they organised their own search, and she says they combed every inch of the area he was working in when he vanished.

"What we found was puzzling, and what did not make any sense in light of what Christopher's co-workers told authorities, was we found one of his boots, his work tools, a blue fibre from his pants and 12 cents on the ground near the items."

"The statements by his employer and co-workers indicated that they believed Christopher just walked off the job site without telling anyone. His other boot was found several months later, miles from the original boot, on some property off I-85." His second boot was found by the owner of the property.

His mother does not believe her son would simply walk away from a job-site, in winter, wearing one or no boots.

His employer apparently said that in the days prior to her son's disappearance he had been acting "strangely." His employer however did not offer any specific details to elaborate on this, and his mother said she was not convinced.

"I saw him every day – he lived with me! There was no strange behaviour, nor any distress."

The Ledger Enquirer wrote in an update a few months afterwards, 'Christopher Carlton Thompkins did not disappear without a trace, but a trace of the 20-year-old is all searchers found when he was last seen Jan. 25, 2002.'

The most obvious explanation about what happened is that hypothetically his co-workers were behind his disappearance. An argument that quickly developed into an altercation. Christopher was somehow flung against the fence, which nicked fibres from his clothing and left them behind when he vanished. He was lifted up somehow during the fight, causing his loose change to fall out of his pocket, he ended up on the other side of the fence, ran, fled, lost a boot, and so on, and yet doesn't that seem a great feat for an assailant or group of assailants to achieve?

How did his boot end up 1.2 miles away? Why was no blood found at the scene? Where did his body go? And, let's just suggest that it was hypothetically the co-workers, the biggest question is, why would they make up such a story about him literally vanishing, within seconds, while he visibly standing among them?

It sounds too fantastical, too otherworldly to believe; or, did something so strange happen to him that they really cannot put it into words?

Was he fleeing something? Something the others did not see? Was he taken right before their eyes...?

Chapter Seven

More Strange Disappearances

In another baffling case, Shannon Schell's mother searched by helicopter over the Rincon Mountains where her daughter disappeared. It was October 1994, when 85 pound 34-year-old Shannon set out alone on a 32 – mile round hike on the Tanque Verde Ridge trail of Saguaro National Monument East to Manning Camp in the Rincon Mountains.

It was to be an over-night trip. Searchers did not feel she set out adequately prepared, as the boots she wore were not hiking boots and they didn't think she had sufficient warm clothing for a night trip that would be cold. They didn't think she had enough water either.

The trail she set out to hike was 8,000 feet of 'vertical mile' from the trail head to Manning Camp, according to Tucson Citizen newspaper. She was also only just recovering from a bout of bronchitis or flu, they said.

'Searchers, including military student volunteers combed the mountain' looking for her after she did not return, searching for her or for any clues to where she had been. Coronado National Forest spokesman Tom Danton said crews were regrouping each evening, 'deciding how to continue the search.'

Carl Bugle, who said he has known Schell for 10 years and had been her boyfriend for the last five years, acknowledged that many things about Schell's disappearance didn't make sense – to someone who didn't know Schell.

'Shannon never held me up,' he said of her mysterious disappearance. In other words, he felt she could easily manage the hike. When questioned about her lack of proper equipment, supplies, and clothing, he said this was down to her confidence – saying she was a very experienced hiker who had been hiking for years. He said she had prepared for this hike for months and had not been planning on going alone but the two friends who had been going with her had unexpectedly pulled out at the last minute.

Authorities said she had got lost once before, in the Santa Ritas for 48 hours but had managed to find her way back out safely. Schell's father, Lee Emmons, said of her trip, "She said it was her challenge.' He added, 'I can't emphasise how resourceful she is,' making it clear that he felt it possible she would be found alive and well. At the time of her disappearance he described her as having 'boundless energy,' and told of her working four jobs to get herself through college. She was now living back with her parents after going through a divorce.

Her mother, having seen the landscape where her daughter had disappeared by helicopter, said, 'There's lots of water up there, seeing all the caves and streams.' She was clinging to the hope that her daughter had found a spot somewhere that she could get water from.

On the day of her disappearance, Schell had parked her

Camaro at the trailhead, locked her wallet inside the trunk and set out on the hike alone. 'She has never been heard from again,' said reporter Vicki Hart of Tuscon Weekly.

'Searchers found a fire ring six miles up the trail with footprints and some items that may have been Schell's, but they never found any trace of Schell herself,' says The Charley Project missing person's website.

During the search for her, there was a very strange twist to the story. Local man Alan Abel told Tucson Citizen, 'We gave the best shot we had,' adding that the effort the National Park Service put in was incredible and he was surprised to see such a high number of people still out voluntarily searching for the missing woman. "There were helicopters and people who had backpacked up there."

The twist came though when a psychic involved him and he conducted a search with his own trained hounds, but hounds which are specifically trained to hunt mountain lions.

'We ran into two fresh sets of lion tracks,' he told reporter Bill Quimby, who points out that his hounds must have been very confused when their master called them off the fresh lion tracks, to try to get them to pick up on the scent of the missing woman, but the reason that the specially trained mountain lion hunting dogs had been taken into the mountain to search for her was because of a vision a psychic had.

It began when Mr. Abel had been returning to the hardware store he owned and found the missing woman's parents standing outside waiting to talk to him. They explained that they had been looking all over town trying to find a man named 'Alan Tools' when eventually they had been directed to his hardware store to ask him. It was now eight days into their daughter's disappearance and the official search had been called off.

A psychic had told the missing woman's parents that they must look for an 'Alan Tools,' because their daughter would be found only be his dogs. The psychic also told them that their daughter was 'still alive and under a rock.' Although his surname is not 'tools' he does of course sell tools at his hardware shop, and the psychic also mentioned the words 'A King of Clubs' as being relevant too.

"It got really spooky," he said. "Although I don't really believe in this stuff – the supernatural, when they wanted to know if I knew anything about 'A King of Clubs' – well, my girlfriend works at 'The King of Clubs,' and the psychic knew my girlfriend's name and other details about us both. I've never even met her!" he said of the psychic, "And she's been getting into my head!"

As chance would have it, when Abel returned to his store and found the parents of the missing girl standing there waiting for him, he'd already been in the midst of preparing his dogs for a lion-hunting trip and his dogs were already loaded. He now planned to trailer the hounds to the trailhead and hunt up.

He and the dogs made a 25-mile return trip from the Ranger Station at Madrona to the Manning Camp, covering extensively the exact route the missing woman had set out on. He and his dogs found nothing, although of course, his dogs were not trained to hunt for lost people, and sadly, whether the psychic was right, and she was still 'alive and under a rock,' he could not find her.

Of course, they would have passed-by thousands upon thousands of rocks in the search for her. What did the psychic mean? Had she fallen under a rock? Had someone placed her under a rock? Or was she hiding from someone or something? Or was the psychic just completely mistaken and only adding to the tragedy? Whichever the case, sadly, she was never found.

"No signs of the woman were found," said Ranger Danton. However, strangely, searchers did find "Cigarette butts of the brand Schell smoked with lipstick matching her shade, throat lozenge wrappers and other debris they are reasonably certain she left behind."

Searchers came across the woman's personal belongings 'in clear view on the trail, neatly bundled in a newspaper sports section, several miles up the most difficult route to Manning Camp.'

The newspaper reports add; 'Oddly, experienced crews covering the same section earlier had not found the items.'

Park Service Ranger and public information officer Tom Danton said, "There are a lot of things that don't make sense,' when asked about this.

~~~~

In October 1998, 36-year-old Robert Michael Bobo disappeared from a remote campground near Woodruff Meadows, between Prospect and Union Creek in the Rogue River - Siskiyou National Forest, Oregon. He was last seen by a female friend who dropped him off at the campsite. When another friend arrived the following morning, for the opening of hunting season, he was nowhere to be found.

The friend discovered he was gone, although his camping gear and other personal belongings were still at his campsite.

According to the records of missing persons organizations, Bobo was last seen on October 2nd,

1998 at approximately 9 p.m. by two hunters in the area. 'Robert Michael Bobo was last seen at his remote campsite outside of Prospect, off Highway 62,' wrote KDRV News in a retrospective. 'Jackson County Sheriff's Office notes Bobo was a transient but had left all of his items at the campsite - describing that as unusual behaviour.'

The Mail Tribune included it in a report on 'the Cold Cases of Jackson County,' and confirmed that he was dropped off and due to be collected the following morning from his remote camp ground but was not found when his friend arrived and looked for him. It's not thought he had much money, as his work as a tree cutter was variable and he also had no means of transport.

Almost two decades later, a cold case investigation team said that DNA samples were taken from his brother to keep on record, presumably should his remains be found, but added that there were new no clues about where Mr. Bobo was, nor what had happened to him. Where he disappeared was heavily wooded.

When he disappeared, the police found no evidence of any foul play, and his case remains open still. The Charley project for missing person's cases writes: 'Authorities stated there were no indications of foul play, but they do not believe Bobo left of his own accord.'

His camp was a heavily wooded spot in the Rogue River - Siskiyou National Park, on the western side of Crater Lake, approximately an hour away from Crater Lake; an area itself that has seen many very strange disappearances of hikers and campers, as well as strange behaviour by hikers or campers.

Since his disappearance, no skeletal remains have been found, no clothes, nothing that could explain what happened to him. His favourite hat, that his family and friends said he would never go anywhere without, has never shown up.

The most disturbing thing perhaps is that his guns were left behind when he vanished. He did not have them to protect himself, wherever he now was.

On the strangeness of the area itself, one very odd story about Crater lake happened back in the 1940's, when a husband and wife were visiting the lake one day. Suddenly, Mrs. Cornelius watched in disbelief and shock as her husband took out his wallet, took off his watch, and handed them to her to hold. Then he sat himself down and pushed himself off a snow chute and slid toward the lake at some speed.

He broke his leg in the inexplicable act, but he didn't stop there. He then crawled to the Lakeshore, entered the water, and drowned himself.

Of course, we do not have details on his mental state nor on any problems he may have been facing in his life, but certainly it would appear a very odd thing to suddenly do.

At Crater Lake and the surrounding area, the unexpected and the unexplained appears to be practically the norm. Over the last century, it has been home to any number of odd disappearances and unexplained vanishings, of both people and planes.

As is often the case in places like this, in the old days, those who were native to the land would do anything they could to avoid going there; particularly the lake area, where the belief and sometimes the experience of the indigenous folk knew that it was wisest to avoid gazing at the lake for too long, and if at all possible, to give it no eye contact whatsoever.

It wasn't a foundless "superstition" that made them like this; it was the overpowering sensation of being drawn to the water, as though being lured closer to the deep blue without any ability to resist.

It was thought to be the pull of the dead spirits, who had returned to cause havoc and entice others to join them in the watery depths. It isn't the first time an area has had this effect on people, but the magnetic effect of the water perhaps somehow compounds this. Often, it's certain cliffs or ridges, but water, with its conducting qualities, perhaps enhances the power.

There is the strange case of a hiker's disappearance in August 2014. Park Officials still don't know what happened that day. The male hiker "eluded a Park Ranger by scrambling down the caldera wall of the ancient volcano." That was the last time anyone saw him, and the Park Service made an appeal to try to find out what had happened to him and to find out if he was ok.

Spokeswoman for the Park, Marsha McCabe said they were not looking for him for a criminal reason, but simply because the path he took was a precarious and highly risky one and they couldn't understand why he would take it, and why he seemed to be fleeing from the Ranger, or from something.

The Ranger had spoken earlier with the man who appeared to be hiking there. Not long after that, the same Ranger saw him scrambling down the caldera by the Lake. The Ranger followed but lost sight of him among the trees. All that was left behind was a pair of sunglasses.

The man was too fast to track and when no sign of him could be found, the park service posted his description on their Facebook page, appealing for information about him. They found his behavior very bizarre and were now worried about his well-being. They said it seemed that after scaling down the caldera, the man had continued along the Pacific Crest Trail. They said he was a white man probably in his '40's with long blonde hair and a beard.

What was surprising to them was his nimbleness and speed, they said, given the fact that he'd been wearing a knee brace on one of his knees and a bandage on the other leg, which stretched from his knee down to his ankle.

How had he been so sprightly? And why was he being so reckless? Had he believed someone or something was chasing him?

Several weeks prior to this another man had hired snowshoes and hiked to the edge of the caldera wall. It was a snow crevice. Then he seemingly vanished. It's quite possible he fell down the caldera wall, about 1,000 feet, and tumbled into the Lake.

Park Spokeswoman Mr. McCabe says a big search effort took place. Boats and divers were used to cover the shoreline area to see if he had gone in the Lake, and meanwhile Search and Rescue tried to track his final journey, but the snow shoe tracks simply stopped. They didn't even find his snow shoes. It was as if he had simply disappeared on the spot.

"It was very, very strange, it's really difficult to get lost in this area; it's such a well-worn and well-marked trail, with lots of hikers on it, so it's really strange that nobody saw him."

~~~~

Fortean researcher in the 1950's, Harold T. Watkins relates an incident in the summer of 1905, in which three young German men from Berlin University, who were students of seismology and petrography, left Husavik, an isolated township of farmers and fishermen on the north-eastern coast of Iceland. They left on horseback to explore the wild region southernly.

It was sunny and bright, and they were in high-spirits, sharing entertaining stories as they rode. After some time, they came to a stop at a small group of farmsteads, where they planned to disembark, and go for a swim in the lake of Odadharhraun. Then they planned to pitch their tent along its sandy shore.

A farmer, whose ancestors had been in this region for three centuries, warned the young men that this lake had an evil reputation. "This place is uncanny," the farmer said, "and in 20 years I have known only 3 people who have ventured in there, and they would not stop there even one night. They returned here, saying they did not like the atmosphere on the shores of the lake where you plan to camp."

"Why?" said the leader of the three Germans, winking at his friends. "What is it about the lake?"

The farmer noted the glances between the Germans, conveying disbelief, and showed that he was annoyed. "All I will say is that the place is uncanny. I and my forebears have lived here more than 300 years and I tell you, young gentlemen, that I, myself, would not spend a night there for 10,000 gilden!"

The German men laughed. "We are students of science, not connoisseurs of old wives' tales. If you mean spooks are there, such things have no place in our philosophy. It sounds interesting. So, a good day to you, mein Herr!"

The three Germans spurred on their horses and rode off laughing at their guide. The farmer knew the region, they did not, and he did not share the light-heartedness of the young men.

In due course, the three Germans reached the shores of the hot lake from which steam rose. They pitched their tent and sent away their native guide with their horses. "Come back in a week's time," the leader told him. "We have food enough to last until then."

The guide, casting a gloomy look on the young men, tied their horses to his crupper and left at a gallop, as if he had a desire to put as much distance as possible between him and the lake before sundown.

Two of the Germans went out on the lake in a

collapsible dinghy. They wanted to gather data on the temperature and depths of the lake. The third man, their 'leader,' walked along the shore examining the rocks and he became absorbed in what he was doing.

About half an hour later, he turned round to look across the lake at his friends. To his amazement, there were no signs of them, or of the dinghy. And the whole lake was visible from shore to shore. Nor could they have landed on the farther bank and wandered inland for he would have seen them and the dinghy.

He shouted repeatedly but all the answer he got in return was the echo of his own voice. Where were his two friends? What had become of them?

He roamed the sandy beach for an hour or more and then as night fell, he went into his tent. He had no ability as a tracker and no map of the region, and he feared that if he tried to follow the track taken by their guide, he would become hopelessly lost in what fortean Watkins calls, 'the fey wilderness,' many miles from habitation.

Says Watkins, 'It may be surmised that he spent a very bad night. Presently, despite himself, he began to fancy that he could see, out of the corner of his eye, shapeless things watching him, and waiting. Fear in its most elemental shape seized him. Against it, none of his science and rationality could prevail.'

'He peered out over the dark and stealthy waters of the lake. He had a rifle and some ammunition and towards midnight he began to fire at shadows in the blackness.'

'All that is definitely known,' says Watkins, 'Is that the guide, when he returned with the horses a week later, found a demented man and had to gallop back for help. A search party was organized, and in a boat, they dragged the lake; but no trace of the missing men or their dinghy was found.'

Sixty miles north-west is Hjeradhsvoton river. One of the lonely villages on its bank is separated from the Church by the waters of this foaming river. Years ago, an old farmer called Oddur Gillasory went across the river to Church one Sunday. He vanished while crossing the river. And he was never seen again, nor his body found. No doubt he fell in and was drowned? Or, maybe he wished to commit suicide?

"Oh no!" say the farmers there. "He just vanished from the sight of those who saw him cross! The river was dragged up and down and he was never seen again...."

~~~~

'Wyoming mountains lured Kent Island man,' wrote staff reporter Dan Fesperman in September 1997. 'Trail likely led to death for missing hiker.'

'The last time anyone saw David Crouch, he was striding across a harsh gray landscape of boulder and crag, well beyond the green comfort of the timberline, and miles beyond the reach of his friends.'

'A few hikers passed in the opposite direction, offering greetings even as they wondered at this unlikely sight so close to sundown - a young man heading up a dead-end trail without a backpack. They said hello. He said nothing. And no one has seen him since.'

The two-week search for athletic 27-year-old David Crouch "has employed helicopters, horses, dog teams and some fifty people. These are certified cadaver-sniffing dogs, so we are not looking for a lost soul up there anymore," said the head of the search organization.

Crouch had not gone out there on the trip alone. Joe Erickson, and his sons Joe Junior and Brad had gone with him. Brad had invited his friend Crouch along. He was a perfect fit for the group, who loved hiking and fly-fishing. Crouch was manager of a bike shop, a runner, long-distance cyclist and sailor.

He wasn't an experienced hiker though, and the group were planning to hike for a week in the Wind River Range of the Bridger National Forest, an isolated spot in Western Wyoming.

Embarking on their trip, they stayed first at an expensive lodge, and were led into the wilderness on horseback with pack horses carrying their supplies. Though they didn't have to struggle carrying their kits, it was a rough ride, across streams and up rocky climbs.

The group reached Moya Canyon that evening, and as they ate super they planed their next day's schedule. They planned to ride a few miles more toward Island Lake, where they would go fishing. Then they would meet up at 2 pm at the Fremont Crossing trail junction for lunch.

The following day, the last sighting of Crouch was as he fished on the South side of the Lake around midday. The next time one of the others in the group looked over at him, he was gone.

At that point no-one panicked – he'd been extremely restless on the trip, they all said later, and it had been a real job to keep him from riding off ahead of them on his own. They all insisted they repeatedly had to warn him not to go off on his own and to all stick together.

They knew the dangers; but they all agreed they had really struggled to get him to listen to them. Really, at this point, they didn't consider him to be missing yet.

When 2 pm came, the others all met up for lunch at the trail junction, but as time passed, Crouch never showed up at their agreed rendezvous point. They waited but Crouch never arrived.

By late afternoon, the group had started searching the Lake and calling out for him. The Lake sits above the timber line, and their voices would carry well.

At this point, despite not locating him, the group were still not too concerned - it happened to be Labor weekend and they figured that, "If he stayed on the trail, other hikers were bound to run across him and he'd be able to find his way back to them,' said Terry

Pollard to the Baltimore Sun. Pollard had been the one to lead them all into the wilderness on horseback and he ran the outfitters shop there.

Bob Reese, District Ranger for the Forest Service, estimated that at least 80 hikers and rock climbers were within a few square miles around the Lake that day. Another local outfitters, Frank Deede, said the number was closer to 140 hikers, which he'd estimated after counting about 40 campsites in the area.

Outfitter Terry Pollard's wife, Barbara, referred to the corridor of trails leading toward the Lake as "the freeway system." In other words, it was very busy there, and she said she passed 45 hikers on one southbound trail alone that day.

In fact, one group of hikers did see him, or someone very much like him. At about 7 pm that evening, the group of hikers were located several miles North East of the Lake, on a trail at 11,000 feet. They said he was heading North, away from the Lake. The trail he was on would end 3 miles further on.

The only way to keep travelling forward then would have been 'only by scrambling across ledges and boulder fields,' says staff reporter Dan Fesperman.

The group who saw him said he was carrying a fishing pole and wearing the clothes his friends described Crouch as wearing when he'd last been seen, so it sounded very much like it was him (although jeans and a plaid shirt is very common clothing, but he fitted the height and build too.)

The group of hikers said they greeted him as they passed him by, saying "Hello," but he didn't reply and just kept on walking.

Outfitter Pollard said their description sounded like it had to be him, but where he was heading and why, he couldn't fathom. "He was way, way off from where he was supposed to be. He must've had some kind of agenda in mind, I guess. I wish I knew…"

If that sighting had been him, as it sounded like it was, he had with him no survival gear, no jacket, no flashlight, no map, no water, no matches.

When the search for him began, tracker dogs picked up a scent in the Lost Lake area, indicating that he had made it back to the location the group had been in the day before they'd gone to the 2nd Lake.

During the official hunt for him, searchers came across a deer that had been killed very recently by a mountain lion. There were no reported sightings of any bears. There was no indication that the missing man had been attacked by natural predators however – there was no torn clothing, no blood, nothing to show something bad had happened to him, and no body.

The dogs would have found him, had he been attacked, but they never found any trace of him….

Where he went and what happened to him, has never been solved.

Chapter Eight

"POSSE SEEKING MISSING WOMAN."

The following strange disappearance happened in the wilderness of Wyoming, nearly a one hundred years ago, and it's the oldest missing person's case in Wyoming. It is still a baffling and unexplained mystery.

In September 1934, a newly-wed young couple went on their honeymoon. For 21-year-old Olga, their destination was the perfect location. She and her husband Carl took off for the wilderness to go Elk hunting. Olga Schultz was a beautiful redhead, who had grown up a country girl. She'd spent much of her life hiking, hunting and fishing.

She had married an oilman called Carl Mauger from Wyoming. In fact, it had been a whirlwind wedding, taking place just weeks after they first met. For their honeymoon, they went to the Togwotee Pass, a mountain pass in the Jackson Hole Valley, situated on the Great Continental Divide in the Absaroka Mountains, 40 miles from Dubois.

Here, they pitched their tent. It was literally in the middle of no-where, although there was a road that ran close-by, but no houses, no stores and no other hunters.

Six days into their trip, they left their camp once more to look for a game trail to hunt Elk; only this time, after they had been hiking for a while, Olga told her husband she was feeling very tired and would like to stop for a rest.

As she sat down to rest for a while, Carl decided to climb the nearby ridge they had planned to climb to "spot" for any Elk. He believed that about twenty minutes passed before he returned to the spot where he'd left his wife at the base of the ridge. Except his wife was no longer sitting there. When he returned, Olga had vanished.

He called out for her and looked all around for anywhere she might have gone, but there really was no-where for her to go other than into the wilderness and that made no sense. She had said she would sit for a while to catch her breath and rest and they had agreed he would just go up on the ridge, very close-by.

When his search for her became futile, he had no other option but to return to their tent. She was no-where to be seen. He could only hope that she must have, for some inexplicable reason, hiked all the way back to their camp alone.

He later said there had been no disagreement between them, no argument and no reason for her not to have waited for him to return to the spot at which she had sat down to rest. But after shouting her name incessantly and turning in all directions to see if he could spot her anywhere in the wilderness, he could not think of anything else that could have happened to her.

When he returned to their camp however, it was empty. The wilderness was very familiar territory for her – she had practically grown up in the wilderness. Being in the wilderness came as second nature to her, so he couldn't imagine she had somehow simply got lost, particularly when she had no reason to take off from her resting place anyway. He sat at the camp, waiting for her to show up, but as the hours passed there was still no sign of her.

Within 48 hours more than 300 people would be scouring the terrain searching for her. The Indian Agency nearby brought their highly skilled trackers in, bloodhounds were brought in, but neither the dogs nor the trackers found any trace of her.

The day she had disappeared she had with her a small bag of sandwiches, a hatchet, and was wearing warm clothing. None of this was found either.

Perhaps inevitably, suspicion strongly pointed at her husband. So much so in fact, that the authorities put him in jail for two months while questioning him on multiple occasions.

According to researcher Robert A. Waters, Olga's sister told reporters that she'd found this passage written down by Olga in her journal. It came from the 'The Rime of the Ancient Mariner,' by English poet Samuel Taylor Coleridge in 1834;

'Like one that on a lonesome road
Doth walk in fear and dread,
And having once turned round, walks on,
And turns no more his head;
Because he knows a frightful fiend
Doth close behind him tread."

But Carl's story never deviated or changed, and the authorities had no solid evidence at all to charge him in the unexplained disappearance of his new wife.

On the other hand, how do we know that the location Carl gave for her disappearance was correct? After all, there was only him and Olga who could vouch for the precise location in which she had disappeared. How do we know she didn't disappear at a different spot, far enough away that the trackers and search dogs would not pick up on her trail?

According to Buckrail, a news and Entertainment site for Jackson and Wyoming; 'Olga was gone without a trace. Some reports say an empty bag of sandwiches was all that remained," while they add rather mysteriously, "Others claim nothing, not even tracks were left behind."

They discovered that Park Ranger KC "Sunny" Allan still remembered getting the call to meet Carl at the Stalnaker hunt camp at 1pm. "A lost lady was reported by Mrs. Angle of Angle's Camp on Togwotee Pass," he wrote in a journal entry. Headlines of the Sunday edition of the Helena Montana, on October 7, (a full month after she vanished) read: "POSSE SEEKING MISSING WOMAN."

Carl told the story to Ranger Allan. 'He said it the same, over and over again to whomever asked. They did not have a fight. There was no reason she would leave intentionally. And Olga was not one to get lost accidentally.'

"Olga was an expert in the forest and everyone knew

she couldn't get lost," the Ranger wrote in the journal.

Ranger Allan had been the one to round up a search party and 300 men joined in the search for the missing woman. This included many members of the Civilian Conservation Corps, game wardens and local men, as well as the expert Indian trackers. When a snowstorm came in, search efforts were impaired, although they had by that time already searched the vicinity several times for the woman.

Carl's own search continued the following year when he was joined by two of Olga's brothers, but they found no body and none of her possessions.

When her husband was in jail for two months, the authorities unravelled the relationship between him and Olga, and others. It seemed that before Carl had married her, he'd been involved with another woman for many years, who had expected him to stay with her forever, but at a dance one night he had caught sight of the beautiful redhead Olga, and from that night onwards he swore to himself that she would be his.

Soon he had dropped his current lover, Ella Tchack, for Olga. There are two versions as to what happened next.

One version is that Ella sent a letter to Carl threatening to kill herself because he had abandoned her. Speculation rose that Carl, overcome with guilt and remorse for leaving Ella, had done away with his new wife so that he could reconcile with his former love. Another version however says that Olga had been sent the letter and upon reading it she had declared she felt guilty enough to kill herself.

However, Olga's sister does not think there was any way in the world that her sister would really kill herself; it just wasn't in her nature, her sister said, but her sister did wonder if Olga had married in haste and now regretted her swift decision to be with Carl. Her sister did say that Olga had practically begged her to join them on her honeymoon. She said that the letter had made Olga very sad.

If anything though, her sister thought Olga may have run away from Carl, using her experience as a talented stenographer to gain employment somewhere. Although they had hiked some miles the day she disappeared, and they were in the middle of the wilderness by foot, Olga had sat to rest on a rock within hearing distance of cars passing by on the Togwotee Pass Road. Had she run off up to the road and hitched it out of there? And yet, her sister cannot understand that if this were the case, why would her sister never contact her family, who loved her and supported her, ever again? Her sister developed a theory that she must have used the excuse of needing to sit down for a rest so that Carl would climb up the ridge alone.

They had both been intending to scale the ridge to look for Elk, but Olga had deliberately pretended to be tired so that he would continue up the ridge alone and give her some precious few moments in which she could escape and run to the road, where she could hitch a ride out of there fast. But if she had run off, she never spoke to her family again, and that did not make sense to them. Why couldn't she simply have divorced her husband, rather than run off into obscurity to start a new life? That is, if she even did really want to leave him.

It's unlikely that a spirited woman such as Olga would have killed herself, thought her family, and they never entertained that theory at all. Had her husband killed her? Had they argued over Ella perhaps, and a fight ensured? But where could he have stored her body, in a place where the Indian trackers and the bloodhounds did not find it?

Seven years after Olga went on that fateful hike in the woods, Carl Mauger obtained a divorce rather than have her declared dead, in kindness of thought to her family, then he married again. His new wife was none other than his former love, Ella.

Did Olga have a terrible accident in the inhospitable wilderness? Did she get up and wander, falling into a gulley or ravine, or off a ridge? But if so, the Indian trackers and the bloodhounds would be sure to have found her. Every inch of the land was repeatedly searched, by 300 men. Even her hatchet was never found. She, and her possessions simply…vanished in the wilderness…

Chapter Nine

GONE

The following disappearance is extremely odd. Linda Arteaga and her brother were visiting relatives in the tiny town of St. Joe, in the Arkansas Ozarks when she and her brother went out for a short hike in the woods. They were last seen leaving their relatives' residence on Highway 374.

"Her brother was going to teach her some survival skills," Shelly Friend, Linda's niece said. It was Saturday, September 22, 2012 when 53-year-old Linda and her 56-year-old brother Eddie Huff left for the woods. Linda was wearing just flip-flops, shorts and a t-shirt.

On Monday 24th, her brother walked out of the woods and told Shelly that her aunt was safe and sitting on the front porch of another relative's house. It wasn't until two days later that her brother realized Linda was in fact still in the woods.

It was explained that the relatives in St Joe live in two separate houses and they do not communicate.

By that Thursday, approximately 100 searchers from at least 10 agencies had joined in the search for the missing woman. They included the County Sheriff's Department, Arkansas State Police, the National Park Service, the Forest Service, the Marshall Police Department and the Office of Emergency Management, as well as a large number of local residents who volunteered. They began to search the woods for her, on foot, horseback and using ATV's.

Fortunately for Linda, the searchers found her after she had survived alone in the woods for five nights. Or, perhaps she wasn't completely alone, as we will get to.

Searcy County Sheriff Kenny Cassell said that when she was found, she was scratched and bruised, but "for five or six days walking around in the woods, she's in great shape." When asked how she had managed to get by all alone in the woods, she apparently said that she had survived on eating any berries she could find, as well as watercress and hazelnuts, and by drinking water from a creek.

Shelly Friend didn't know if they would find her aunt alive. The teams of police and emergency staff called it a "search and recover" mission, not "search and rescue," newspapers reported. "You understood they were looking for a body, not a survivor, and that's what we were kind of expecting," said her niece.

The Sherriff said, "She told me the flip flops blew out the first day."

When she was asked about why she had been left behind in the woods by her brother, who had said he was teaching her survival skills, she said she could not recall exactly what had happened after becoming separated from her brother.

She said she felt that he was somehow hurt and that she had gone off to seek help for him, although her brother, who had returned home, bore no injuries at all.

A crying Linda told Sheriff Cassell that she had to sleep on a bed of rocks. Deputy sheriff Dewayne Pierce said, after her rescue; "She wasn't quite about her head."

Most strangely, she said that in her search for people to help her brother, she had come across other people in the woods but that all efforts to communicate with these people had proved fruitless. She said that despite her trying to talk to them, they had all appeared to act as if they could not hear her nor see her. None of them responded to her at all.

"I'd ask for help, and they'd act like they didn't even hear me!"

She described herself as being "very scared" and her plight as "freaky," saying; "These people were hiding in bushes. They were weird people, very weird people."

Even more ominously, she said that she also saw "shadowy figures" lurking in the bushes and behind trees.

Some tried to rationalize her story by saying she was hallucinating from the berries she was eating to survive.

Medical Director of NARMC's Hospitalist Program said, "Whatever she experienced, whether or not it was real or hallucinary, she clearly did experience that."

Dr. John Sorg, of North Arkansas Regional Medical Centre said, "I suppose she could have had some toxic ingestion that may have caused a hallucinogen; but you know, she's been very consistent with that story, and today in her mental examination, she seems very oriented and appropriate in conversation." In other words, he didn't think these were hallucinations.

Her tale is very reminiscent of accounts in several of my other books in this series, where the lost can see the searchers, and yet somehow it seems that the searchers cannot see the lost.

It is somewhat like the strange story of Mohd Ghani, a 15 year old who vanished for eight days in 2008 on Gunung Tebu, a thick forested mountain region 1039 above sea level in Jerith, Malaysia.

The Utusan Newspaper reported, "Mohd was found today in a place that had been repeatedly searched by the search party, triggering a mystery that has confounded police. Even Mohd wonders how the search team and volunteers and even his own mother did not see him when he was in that same area since he had been reported missing."

The boy himself said, "During the period the search parties and people were searching for me, I came across the search party. I heard my mother call but I couldn't do anything..."

It appears that he never left the area in which he had disappeared and was then subsequently found 8 days later; he was there all the time; but the searchers couldn't see him even though he could both hear them and see them, and he could clearly see his mother searching for him.

The Newspaper wrote, 'State police Chief Lub Hussain expressed complete astonishment because the boy was found only 8 metres from the bridge on which he had last been seen.'

The Police Chief himself said, "I was quite surprised that after all the places we were looking for him, behold, he was at the center of the public eye, by the river, and the funny thing is he's still in good health and showed no signs of fatigue."

More than 130 rescuers had been searching for 8 days for him, including the police, the army, and the People's Volunteer Corps. All the villagers nearby had joined in. None of them could find a trace of the missing boy, until eight days had passed, and then he was there, standing by the river, yet oddly, he was no longer wearing clothes; he had on just a towel, wrapped around his waist, and he was standing there, just gazing out over the river.

The boy, a boy scout himself, could not explain how he came to be wearing the towel, nor why he says he had been "hanging around the area the whole time," and yet no-one had been able to see him there..

~~~~

The Philadelphia Daily News reported on May 7th, 1979, that a Steven Kubacki, 24, had returned home after being reported missing fifteen months earlier. 'HOME UNHARMED,' said the Hutchinson Daily News.

Steven Kubacki had just walked into his aunt June Bozak's home in Great Barrington in Berkshire County, Massachusetts. He was unhurt but claimed he was suffering from amnesia. A student at Hope College in South Haven, Michigan, Steven had been presumed lost and no longer alive after setting out on a cross-county ski trip alone along the shore of Lake Michigan.

After he didn't return and was reported missing, Michigan State Police went out searching for him. They came across his skis and poles and saw that his footprints led across the Lake Michigan ice for approximately 200 yards, then stopped.

Helicopters, dogs and foot patrols turned up no trace of him. When the ice thawed, more searches were carried out but again they found no trace of the man. It was presumed that he must have fallen through the ice and drowned (although there was no obvious hole in the ice to show this).

After giving up the searches for him, the Police even sent his dental records to Chicago authorities to see if he might have been among the bodies found at the home of suspected serial killer John Wayne Gacy, but that also turned up no evidence.

The student's father said of his son's return, "I'm very happy. I'm not pressing him too hard for details, but he says he stopped on Saturday in a town and asked a passer-by, "What place is this?" He was told he was in Pittsfield, Western Massachusetts."

"That triggered something. I don't know why, but things then started coming back to him. The past just came back to him."

He got in touch with his aunt, who called family members. "He doesn't remember anything else." his father said. He said his son was disoriented and "he didn't even know what year it was."

Kubacki's mother said her son appeared to be in good health. "Whatever it is, I don't care. I don't have any explanations - I don't need one."

Where had he been in all that time? Had he suffered from extreme concussion? Some say it was as if he must have entered an alternate dimension.

Chapter Ten

Missing Genius

On May 29th, 1999, the remains of Philip Taylor Kramer were found. The one-time bass guitarist for the group 'Iron Butterfly' had been missing for four years. His death is a mystery to this day.

His 1993 Ford Aerostar van was found at the bottom of a Malibu Ravine by hikers in a canyon about 1.5 miles east of the Pacific Coast Highway. His remains were found inside his van and identified through dental records.

His death would ultimately be ruled "probable suicide," however his family hold strong doubts about this. His widow told the La Times, "He would never under any circumstances for any reason allow himself to completely abandon the family he loves more than life itself."

Kramer had been bass player in the psychedelic group 'Iron Butterfly,' recording albums in the mid '70's. By 1977 however, he decided to refocus on furthering his education, and he completed a degree in Aerospace engineering. He was highly intelligent, having got straight A's all through School and once gaining his degree he went to work for Northrup, working on the MX missile guidance system as a Department of Defense contractor.

Sometime later, he made a move into the computer industry, where he worked on facial recognition and communications development programs. He was quite possibly a computer genius.

On February 12th, 1995, he'd driven to LA Airport where he was due to pick up a business colleague and his wife. However, after approximately 45 minutes, he got back into his car and left the airport without waiting for his colleague to arrive.

He stopped after a while and made a series of strange telephone calls. He called a former band member and good friend, Ron Bushy, and said to him, "I'll see you on the other side." Then he called the police and said, "This is Philip Taylor Kramer. I'm going to kill myself. And I want everyone to know O.J Simpson is innocent. They did it." Then he disappeared.

His vanishing remained a mystery until his skeletal remains were found in his car, 48 months later. How did he wind up at the bottom of Decker Canyon, of which the magazine Maxim wrote, "If you ever need to dump a corpse, you could do worse than Dekker Canyon. Located a 40-minute drive from LA, the rugged chasm is all but uninhabited. Best of all there's a thick screen of trees at the bottom. All you have to do is prop up the body in the front seat, release the parking brake and let em rip..'

His skeleton was discovered by 30-year-old Walter Lockewood, a fitness instructor and amateur photographer with a penchant for taking pictures of old abandoned cars. He'd heard stories over the years of cars being driven off the cliff there, and he'd ventured to the canyon to see if he could find any, thinking they would make cool photographs.

He'd taken a friend with him and that afternoon they had climbed down the canyon. Quickly, despite the over-grown trees and bushes, they spotted an abandoned pick-up truck, then further on a sedan. It began to give them the creeps – there was nothing glamorous about the cars now – they were violently smashed up.

Then they spotted another vehicle partly hidden in the undergrowth. There were no plates on it. The Aerostar van was smashed in on the driver's side and it looked like it had come down off the cliff head-first. An overpowering stench hit them. They thought they could see a leg bone.

They didn't want to stay any longer, thoroughly horrified by it, and they left to summon the police. As they walked through a gully, they saw a human skull – which would turn out to be the missing rock musician-turned computer genius.

Intriguingly, 'He was a brilliant scientist who played with mathematics formulas for fun! Yet he also believed he was in telepathic communication with aliens,' Maxim Magazine wrote.

According to his friend Bushy, although the other band members had been into drugs and women, Kramer had eschewed this traditional Rockstar style in favor of long-nights spent on mathematical puzzles.

Said Bushy, "We'd stay up all night, write music and talk about his theories. He was talking stuff that was science fiction – about how you could not only communicate but also transport matter from A to B anywhere in the galaxy! Real beam me up stuff!"

Other records show that in the days before he disappeared, he had been supposedly working on perfecting a top-secret 30-year-old formula that he and his father believed would disprove Einstein and change the course of history. The formula was based on a theory that linked faster-than-light communications.

'It was a kind of gravitational vibration wilder than anything seen on Star Trek. It was, he believed, worth billions, and then, one day, he disappeared, leaving behind a web of suspicion, intrigue and conspiracy theories more elaborate than anything since the grassy knoll.'

His obsession for theoretical mathematics and physics began as a child when his father was professor of Engineering at Ohio State University. His father Ray, in the early 60's, had begun a driven theoretical quest to conquer the boundaries of time and space.

His father claimed, "Using the formula I discovered, you could reach the outer limits of the universe in less than a second." Now retired, he is less outspoken. Wrote Maxim he 'remains extremely secretive about his research,' although 'in passing he'll casually take credit for inventing weather radar.'

'His greatest achievement he says, is his Universal Equation which promises to solve physics most intractable mysteries – a meta-theory that ties together black holes, quarks, and quantum mechanics into an all-encompassing package. He says, with it, information can be transmitted 16 times the speed of light – a potentially earth-shattering achievement that conventional science says is impossible.'

Kramer's friend Bushy says the professor's son wanted to finish his dad's research into space and time, and he transformed himself from rock music and late nights into the serious job of working on guidance missiles as a Department of Defense contractor at Northrop. He worked under 'top secret' clearance.

In those days, his cubicle had to be taped shut when he was in it – so people would know they could not cross the boundary, as was common practice back then.

The precise details of exactly what he did, of course, is still classified. Then he moved on from this position to branch out on his own, and while marrying and having a daughter, he set up a company that would turn music into digital form – developing a fractal data compression technology for CD-ROMs using a new technique. Sadly, he lacked the financial support despite having a brother of Michael Jackson as an investor, and the start-up company went bankrupt.

That's apparently when things started to get strange. Says Maxim, 'A new COE, Peter Olsen made 'The Celestine Prophecy', 'a book that asserts that enlightened people vibrate at such a high frequency they disappear,' virtually mandatory reading, and declared himself to be a New-Ager.

'Word circulated among some employees that he proudly declared himself to be half-human half-alien.'

Kramer's sister Kathy said her brother too soon began to claim he 'Spoke frequently with aliens.'

In February 1995, his father helped him with something that had been driving him crazy – he'd been working night and day obsessively trying to combine data compression with gravity waves for communication systems when his father suggested he should apply their 'theory' to it.

This led to a Eureka moment – and, apparently many more long days and nights of feverish work by Kramer, interspersed by Kramer phoning family and friends to declare that something really "amazing" was happening.

However, those around him were growing concerned that he wasn't sleeping. According to his wife, he was finding 'sacredness' in everything. He warned his wife he might be in danger. He told good friend Lori Pietsch that he now had to be very careful.

He told her; "People are going to want what I'm working on. We have to get off the planet. I was able to decipher the code – it was heavily encrypted."

It was shortly after this that he was due to meet a business college and their wife at LA airport. Instead, he left the airport without picking them up, phoned his wife and told her he had a big surprise, phone his best friend to tell him he loved him, then dialed 911 and told them he was going to kill himself.

Was this a clear-cut case of mental exhaustion and

resulting delusion? Had his new-age reading about aliens and transcendence spurred his imagination into overdrive? Or, had he discovered something so shocking and secret that mere mortals could not be allowed to know it, and there was a human hand in keeping this secret quiet?

He called his wife and told her he was not going to see her "on this side." In other words, it would seem he meant that they would meet again in Heaven, after death.

Then he stopped off to see his father-in-law, who was terminally ill. He pulled a small viewing device from his pocket – which turned out to be a child's toy with a lens that fragmented and replicated anything it viewed, and he told his father-in-law, "It's all right here. I know you don't understand - but it's all right."

Strangely, his father said his son had told him that if he were ever in trouble, he would call 911 and tell them he was going to kill himself. His father said this was a coded message to say that he was under the control of others. But how would everyone get this message, one has to ask? Why wouldn't he phone his father or wife directly with a coded message?

Friend Lori Pietsch, who he had told, "I was able to decipher the code - people are going to want what I'm working on. We have to get off the planet," said, 'I'm convinced he was under mind control or psychic attack."

"Something happened during that time – either in his head or at the terminal – that made him turn away," said former L.A. police officer Chuck Carter, who worked on the case. "Whatever happened in his head at the airport, or whatever happened right in the airport, I've got a feeling we'll learn from Kramer himself."

After he didn't return home, a woman and her daughter said they saw him at a garage sale a few weeks later. His sister Kathy said she's not convinced it was even his body they found.

When he went missing, The Washington post asked; 'Is

Kramer trapped by his own technological wizardry, imprisoned somewhere in cyberspace?' Many people believe that when Kramer vanished he entered another realm.'

Mainstream physicists however said he and his dad's theories involving hyperparticles and gravity and hyperspeed were folly. What they said could be achieved simply wasn't possible, according to these experts.

Although Kramer seemed to be greatly over-worked when he vanished, and very possibly beginning to lose his grip on reality, he had no history of psychiatric problems neither did he take drugs or drink. It was believed the company he had founded was probably struggling in debts; but he was a devoted family man, not someone people believed would walk out on his wife and daughter.

He was working late into every night prior to his disappearance however, and was prone to outbursts such as, "God is a scientist. A perfect scientist! Chaos is perfect order!"

The day before he vanished he told his sister "You've got to be centered. If you're centered, you'll be saved when the supernova happens, and they come." His sister went on any TV show that would have her, to publicize his strange disappearance.

He also told his wife they'd have to move into a house with high walls. "He was scared that people were trying to get at him," she said.

He said he had channeled the Tenth insight from The Celestine Prophecy and he had called a friend to transcribe it for him as he channeled it.

After he disappeared, his family hired a private eye, friends searched everywhere they could think of, and local congressman James Traficant apparently sent a letter to the FBI urging an immediate investigation. He felt that there was 'the possibility that foreign elements could be involved' and he urged an analysis of the 911 call be made to determine if Kramer had made the call voluntarily, or perhaps under duress.

Because of the former classified work he had done as a Defense contractor, and because of the material he was now working on, the congressman wondered, could foreign factions be after his knowledge?

His best friend Bushy said, 'After his breakthrough, we wouldn't need cell phones, landlines, or satellites' – and he implied big business could be behind his vanishing.

According to the Washington Post, Glen Mavis, who worked with Kramer back at Northrop said, "Whatever got him was something that he couldn't deal with – whether it was an outside force that came down on him or ….."

Detective Tom Bennett, who handled the case for Ventura Sheriff's Department said; "There's some funny things here…Officially the case is still open…."

"Chaos is perfect order!" Kramer had announced prior to his disappearance, "I was able to decipher the code - it was heavily encrypted. People are going to want what I'm working on. We have to get off the planet…"

What did happen to Philip Kramer?

'In his head he carried secrets, some said to be of incalculable value,' said The Washington Post.

What were these secrets?

Chapter Eleven

Strange Encounters

Back in the 1930's, Steve Brodie was an artist and keen rock collector. One day, he and a friend headed out into the Superstition Mountains to search for quartz crystal rocks.

Despite being fully-briefed by some local people about the reputation of people mysteriously disappearing in the Superstition mountains outside of Phoenix Arizona, Brodie decided that this would not deter them one bit. He knew there were good crystals in the mountains and he wanted to find them. What subsequently happened to him, he related to UFO researcher John J. Robinson, twenty years later.

When they went to the mountains, they set their sights on one particular bluff where they believed the most exciting crystals would be found. However, as soon as they reached the base of this bluff, he said, a hooded figure came out from the shadow of the rocks. As Brodie and his friend froze in shock, the shrouded figure raised an arm and pointed a long device at Brodie's friend, and his friend appeared to fall to the floor and lie motionless, apparently appearing to have been killed.

The hooded figure then came toward Brodie, who was standing frozen in shock, and placed some kind of device over his head, like a metal helmet with two discs that covered either side of his temple. Brodie then believes he lost consciousness, as the next thing he saw was a dungeon or underground cave in which he was now standing and he found himself surrounded by other humans.

All of the other humans being held prisoner in the underground dungeon appeared to be in some kind of trance-like state, which veered from comatose to sometimes slightly-awake. Brodie recalls rousing himself too on occasion, and in one instance he managed to communicate with a female prisoner, asking her where they were.

The female prisoner replied that they were being held captive by the 'Dero,' but she did not explain where their prison was.

His recollection of his time in the underground prison was scant and though he struggled to describe more, he could not, until he found himself wandering the streets of New York City, with absolutely no idea how he got there.

When he finally made it back home, his new artwork seemed to begin to be influenced by his underground experience. He now found himself painting out-of-this-world landscapes never seen before. His entire painting style was now different. He wasn't even aware of what he was painting or at least he had no plan to paint what he ended up painting.

It was at this time that he got into a conversation with his neighbour, Robinson, the UFO researcher. Brodie had gone to see Robinson and when they were chatting in Robinson's apartment, his eyes fixed upon a magazine in the lounge, called 'Amazing Stories.' In this magazine was a story about someone's experiences with a race of beings called 'The Dero' and on seeing the article headline across the front page of the magazine, Brodie suddenly shouted out: "He speaks of the Dero!!"

It was then that he began to confide in Robinson about his horrifying experience in the Superstition Mountains and of finding himself a prisoner underground until sometime later he was wandering aimlessly along a busy New York sidewalk.

Robinson noted the once hyper-relaxed artist now expressed a high level of paranoia, frequently stating that he believed he was being followed and observed. Robinson visited him several times to hear his accounts of the time he had been held underground by the mysterious figures in black hoods, but one day when he returned once more to visit Brodie, Brodie was not there. He had gone, and he was never seen again.

No-one seemed to be able to tell Robinson where he had gone or what had happened to him. One neighbour claimed they had seen him one time in the Arizona desert wandering like a zombie.

A man called Richard Shaver, also claimed to have had his run-ins with the Dero race. He claimed that the "voices" he heard were coming from below the ground, where warring alien species were battling each other. These entities he called 'The Dero' and 'The Tero' races; which he claimed, with their advanced technology were capable of transmitting electronically-enhanced telepathic brain waves.

He said he'd been taken to the underground, led there by a holographic image of a 'being,' through a hidden entrance. The 'Deros' were planting thoughts in his head to make him sound ridiculous, he said, so that no-one would believe what he said about the existence of these underground bases and to prevent the public from taking him seriously, because the Deros feared their bases were soon going to become public knowledge.

According to Shaver, the 'Deros' kidnapped people from

above ground by the hundreds and took them below, to use them for meat.

He said this species were capable of causing accidents, disasters and illnesses to people, and that they already exerted incredible power over the unsuspecting general public, who did not know they were being systematically mind-controlled remotely.

The editor of the magazine 'Amazing Stories,' who interviewed Shaver, claimed he heard several different voices emanate from Shaver as he talked aloud, and that chillingly, the voices were discussing the murder of a woman in one of the underground bases.

~~~~

This next story is extremely unsettling; One misty night in the winter of 1974, 68-year-old Mr. William Bosak of Frederic, Wisconsin had what he described as 'a hair-raising experience.'

He was driving carefully home to his rural dairy farm, where he'd lived for over 30 years, in the fog after a farmer's meeting when he suddenly saw a strange object on the road side. As he drove closer to it, what he saw baffled his mind and defied any logical explanation.

He would later tell newspapers that it was a human being standing inside a bullet-shaped transparent glass compartment.

This figure inside the glass compartment was between eight and ten feet in height, he said, and 'his' arms were raised above his head. The man's ears were higher on his head than was normal.

"I was so goldarned scared, I was afraid to go out at night," he told reporters. The figure, he said, was wearing a tight-fitting suit, but had a furry-upper body.

"He was looking out the window. It was a different kind of character than you'd see on this earth - It looked a good deal like a man, but it had a different-looking face. It had a kind of a cow-looking face," he said, reports W-Files.com. "His ears were shaped like cow's ears too." The being had no collar or shirt but did appear to be dressed!

As he drove away from the strange creature in the glass tank, the inside of his car got dark and he heard a noise like the engine was missing. He also heard a soft whooshing sound, like tree branches rubbing up against a car.

Investigator Everett E. Lightner reported that Bosak was very frightened at the time, but the look on the alien's face looked as scared as he was. He could tell by its large eyes protruding from his head!

Though the driver was terrified of it, he also regretted leaving it; "I should have stopped and tried to show it I was friendly - I wish I could meet up with it again." Source: Why-files, ufoevidence.org, thinkaboutitdocs.com

The newspaper account appeared in the St. Paul Pioneer-Press, though the farmer kept it to himself for a month or so at first. "I'll take a lie detector test to prove this isn't just something I made up," he told reporters.

Lightner, who investigated the case, found the farmer to be held in good regards by all who knew him in the farming community, and none had a bad word to say about him, leading the investigator to believe he was being sincere about his encounter....

∼∼∼∼

In November 1896, the Stockton Evening Mail of California published a very strange account from a Colonel H.G. Shaw, who says that he was in a horse and carriage traveling along a country road near Lodi, in San Joaquin County California, with a friend named Mr. Camille Spooner when they found themselves harassed by three tall, thin humanoids, who attempted to kidnap the Colonel and his friend. The Colonel said that fortunately they successfully managed to fend these strange humanoids off.

'THREE STRANGE VISITORS Who Possibly Came From the Planet Mars, Seen on a Country Road by Colonel H.G. Shaw and a Companion,' said the newspaper. Of the Colonel, the newspaper says, 'The gentleman was very reticent about relating the circumstance, as he said he had no idea that it would believed by anyone, and he was loath to appear before the public.'

The Colonel says, 'Were it not for the fact that I was not alone when I witnessed the strange sight I would never have mentioned it at all. The horse suddenly stopped and gave a snort of terror. We beheld three strange beings. They resembled humans in many respects but still they were not like anything I had ever seen.'

'We were startled, as you may readily imagine, and the first impulse was to drive on. However, the horse refused to budge. The group of beings were at least 7 feet tall, and extremely thin.' In fact, the Colonel estimated their weight to be less than 1 ounce, which is far less than a bag of sugar.

'They were communicating with each other with "warbling" sounds, like "a monotonous chant" that was "guttural" too. Their feet were long and narrow, and their toes were as long as fingers.' silk and soft as velvet. They had no hair. Their ears were tiny and their noses like 'polished ivory.' Their eyes were very large.

Their mouths were tiny, "and it seemed to me they were without teeth,' said the Colonel.

'We concluded to get out and investigate. I asked where they were from. They seemed not to understand me. Their remarks were addressed to each other, "warbling" better than talking. Like a monotonous chant. I saw it was no use to attempt conversation.'

'They seemed to take great interest in ourselves. They scrutinized everything. Their feet were nearly twice as long as an ordinary man. Their fingers were without nails. They were seven feet and very slender. They were without any clothing. The mouth was small and without teeth; that, among other things led me to believe they neither ate nor drank and that life was sustained by some sort of gas. Each had a bag under the left arm to which was attached a nozzle.'

'One or the other every little while would place a nozzle on his mouth and I heard the sound of escaping gas; the same sound as blowing up a football. Each held to his hand something about the size of an egg. These substances emitted the most remarkable, intense and penetrating light one can imagine.'

'One of them came close to me. I reached out to touch him. It was soft as silk to the touch. Placing my hand under his elbow I lifted him from the ground with scarce effort. The gravity of the creature was less than one ounce.'

'I do not want you to get the idea these creatures were hideous. They were the contrary. They were possessed of a strange and indescribable beauty. They were graceful, and more divinely beautiful than anything I ever beheld.'

'Finally, they became tired of examining us, and then one of them, at a signal from one who appeared to be the leader, attempted to lift me, probably with the intention of carrying me away. He could not move me, and finally the three of them tried it without success.'

'They appeared to have no muscular power outside being able to move their own limbs.'

The beings then flashed their lights, and resting in the air about twenty feet above the nearby river the Colonel noticed 'an immense airship.' It was 150 feet in length at least, and outside of a large rudder there was no visible machinery.

'They walked rapidly toward the ship, not as you or I walk, but with a swaying motion, their feet only touching the ground at intervals of about fifteen feet. We followed as rapidly as possible. With a spring they rose to the machine, a door opened and disappeared within. It went through the air very rapidly, as it expanded and contracted with a muscular motion, and soon was out of sight.'

The newspaper adds, 'For more than a week, the papers all over the coast have been reporting the presence of an alleged flying machine, which many reputable people claim to have seen on several occasions in the heavens at night.'

The 'beings' that tried to abduct the Colonel did not succeed, they were not strong enough, but what if, in the century between this encounter and now, they have grown stronger?

~~~

In Wales in 1887, as recorded by the Reverend Elias Owen and published in a prize essay of the National Eisteddfod in 1896, and later in 'Encounters of the Unexplained' by Marcus Day, the Reverend recorded details of a manservant of his Mother.

The manservant, called David Williams, was used to accompanying the Reverend's mother, a widow, home from her travels to neighbours and friends. This particular evening, he was walking her safely home from an evening at her friends' house in Tyddin Heilyn in Penrhyndevdreath, near the river.

David was a trusted manservant and when she walked home with him in the darkness she had always felt safe and secure, given that David's nickname was "Big David" on account of him being very tall and broad and sturdy and strong.

This evening, he was carrying a big slab of pork over

his shoulders and he walked deferentially a couple of steps behind his employer.

The Reverend's mother made her way back home, not feeling the need to glance behind her at all, to check that he was there, ss he was always there, just behind her. So, she had no cause to doubt his presence.

In due course, she arrived back home and at that point, she turned around to thank him, only to find that he was no-where to be seen. To her shock, she could not see him anywhere in the darkness and she couldn't understand it.

Too unsettled to go to bed, she sat waiting for him, wondering where on earth he could be, but it wasn't until three long hours had passed that he arrived, still carrying the slab of pork on his shoulder.

When she asked him where he'd been he expressed confusion, telling her that he had been right behind her, and had arrived back home now, just a minute or so behind her.

She questioned him again, not able to understand why he wasn't telling her the truth, as he clearly had not been right behind her, and eventually he admitted that something very strange had happened to him. What he went on to tell her next was most bizarre.

He told her that as he had been walking behind her through the fields, he had suddenly seen a dazzling meteor flying through the night sky, and that behind this meteor was a hoop of fire with a tiny man and a tiny woman standing inside of it. They were holding onto each other and both had hold of the hoop of fire too.

The hoop of fire then descended into the field and when it touched the ground, the two little people jumped out of the hoop, and began to create a circle in the field. As soon as they had created their make-shift circle, lo and behold a group of tiny fairy-folk appeared out of no-where and entered the circle, which was now bathed in soft light and they began to dance to the sound of the most beguiling music. It was the most entrancing music the manservant had ever heard.

At some point after this, he said the meteor returned, collected the small man and woman and zoomed fast back up into the sky. The group of dancing fairies, he said, vanished into thin air shortly afterwards.

Alone again, the manservant made his way back to the Reverend's mother's house, completely in shock at what he had just witnessed.

He thought that the duration of the bizarre incident had lasted for just minutes or seconds; little did he know that he had been there watching, and perhaps more, for three hours.

Even stranger, how did he see all of this and yet the widow did not, when he had been only a step or two behind her?

If we are to believe his sincerity (and it would be a crazy story to make up and tell an employer, whom his livelihood depended upon), so if he was telling the truth, how did this happen without her also seeing the meteor?

Is this how easily one person can have an experience, seemingly of supernatural origin, and disappear, when just a step or two away from another person, who is fortunate enough not to be the one who is taken or 'disappeared?' How could this happen?

~~~~

Retired Assistant Police Commander Brian Langston writes on mysteries, crime, and the paranormal on http://www.brianlangston.com/.

He discovered 'a long-forgotten pamphlet lying in a dusty corner of the reading room of the British Museum, telling the incredible tale of how, during the late 17th century, a young man in North Cornwall was mysteriously teleported 30 miles from his home by an unknown force.'

The young boy in question was Jacob Mutton, a servant employed by the Rector of Cardinham, William Hicks, who lived on Bodmin Moor in Cornwall, England. Bodmin Moor is in the county of Cornwall, on England's rugged southwestern tip. The Moor is a designated Area of Outstanding Natural Beauty, and is a remote, bleak heather-covered granite moorland of 208 square kilometres.

The servant boy was apparently deemed to be an honest and hard-working employee by the Rector and all others who knew him. The event that happened apparently occurred sometime after 8 pm on Sunday 8th May 1687. It was then that the servant boy took himself off to bed in the Rectory. He shared the bedroom with another servant boy, who was at the time already in bed.

He later explained that as he began to get undressed for bed he began to hear a voice which he described as 'hollow,' and this voice was saying, "So Hoe, So hoe, so hoe.." It sounded as though the voice was coming from a nearby room, and so the servant boy went off to investigate. In this room, he could hear the voice again, but it sounded as if it was coming from outside the windows.

The young boy peered out of the windows, but he could see nothing outside. The last memory he had was of watching out of the window, until the following morning, when he was found lying unconscious in a countryside lane by folks travelling to market at Stratton Fair.

As they roused him, he appeared to be completely baffled about what he was doing lying in the country lane, in a spot he did not recognise. He was approximately 4 miles from the town of Bude and 30 miles from his home.

The travelling group couldn't just leave him there all alone and confused, and so they took him with them to the market at Bude, for the Stratton Fair. Once the Fair was over, the group set him on the right road to make his way back home, now a distance from the Fair of 20 miles, where he was eventually discovered by other travellers and taken to spend the night in Camelford.

The following morning, he continued his journey on foot alone and eventually arrived back home at the Rectory the following day, having walked all night to get home. Fortunately, he had made it home in one piece and physically looked no worse the wear for it. However, the Rector noticed that his demeanour appeared changed.

He was very quiet, and he appeared sad. This was not the usual behaviour of this normally cheerful boy. Mind you, he had just walked thirty miles! But this demeanour continued as the days passed.

The Rector of course was concerned about where Jacob had been all this time, and when he asked his servant boy, all Jacob could explain was that a 'tall man' had taken him 'over hedges...without weariness or hurt,' but he could not say what happened to his companion, the 'tall man.'

"There the story ends....." says Brian Langston. 'Through a 21st century lens, the story sounds remarkably like an early account of alien abduction although of course such phenomena had not then been identified and the language simply did not exist to describe the experience he underwent."

"The brevity of the account is fascinating, frustrating and leaves many unanswered questions. Is it relevant that the incident took place on the mysterious Bodmin Moor - a place closely associated with strange happenings across the centuries? Why was he left there? Who was the mysterious stranger who took Jacob?"

~~~~

Anthropologist Carmen Blacker studied ancient oral and written lore of Japan for her paper 'Supernatural Abductions in Japanese Folklore.' One oral tale she discovered was the story of a child in a small rural village in the Aichi region who vanished on the evening of September 30th, 1907.

Everyone was busy preparing white rice cakes to be given as offerings to the gods at a festival the following day. When it was discovered that the child was missing, a search was begun for him, but by the next day he still had not been found. When the festival was over, and celebrations had quieted down, an even more thorough search effort continued all across the village and in the fields and woods, but they still found no sign of the boy and no indication to explain what might have happened to him.

Then, all of a sudden, a loud thud was heard on the roof of the house the boy lived in. Some of the villagers climbed up onto the roof to find out what had caused the thud and to their surprise they discovered the missing boy, laying prone and unconscious.

When they finally managed to rouse him, he told them that he had been standing underneath the large cedar tree when a stranger had appeared and taken him away. He said they had walked over treetops until eventually he found himself thrust into a tiny place – which turned out to be the roof of his own house. After his odd experience, the boy's mind was said to have never recovered.

Blacker also relates another incident featuring an older boy who lived in the Kumano district. It was a century earlier, on the night of the 19th of May, when he got out of bed to go to the lavatory. He did not return. His family, aware that he had gone into the lavatory and not come back out, searched the lavatory, his bedroom, and then everywhere else in the house but could not find him.

They searched outside, and their search continued for hours until they discovered him standing on the eaves of the roof, the top of his hair cut off and his clothes covered with grass.

His parents put him to bed and they said that he slept for three weeks then woke to explain what had happened to him. He said that a mountain man had appeared, taken him by the hand and flown them up into the sky. He said they had flown for a great distance, at amazing speed, stopping here and there on mountain tops.

He said he had a marvellous time and would like to have seen more places but he worried for his family and so he returned. He said he had been returned home in one big leap.

Another story comes from an 18th century collection called 'Kaidan Tōshiotoko.' A young boy set out from his house in the Sanuki province to go on an errand for his mother. Some peasants working in the fields noticed him and they watched him with curiosity as he diverted off the dirt path he was walking on and began to run through the fields of wheat.

They shouted out to him angrily, asking him why he was trampling their crops, but the little boy gave no answer and then simply disappeared. He was running through the field and simply vanished in front of their eyes.

When they realized he had not fallen into the crops and become hidden, and they could not see him anywhere, they eventually went in concern and alarm to his mother's house, to tell her that her son appeared to have gone missing.

His mother was understandably shocked, and in fear of what had happened to him, she and her neighbours and all of the village turned out in search of him, continuing on well after it got dark, and their search continued through the following day and night, desperately trying to find him but he was not in the fields and he was nowhere else either.

Each night, the villagers would bang on drums and ring bells, to alert the boy that they were searching for him, until finally, after many days of this, they eventually gave up searching for him. They had searched everywhere and found no sign of him at all, nor any clues as to what had happened to him in the field that day.

Then, suddenly, he was spotted, standing on the altar of the local Temple not far from the village. The villagers who found him took him straight home to his mother, but he lay unable to speak and seemed to be unconscious in bed for several days. When finally he regained his ability to talk, everyone asked him what had happened to him on the day he was seen running through the field of crops.

He replied that "two Yambushi seized him and pulled him by the hand, away to many places until finally they let him rest on the top of Mount Yakurigatake. Here, he said three more ''Yamabusi' joined them.

Yamabushi, according to Japanese esoteric mysticism

are monk-like hermits believed to have supernatural powers. The boy said they played music for him and tossed him up into the air, playing games with him, until an old priest came to them and told them to let him go and to hand over the boy. The boy could remember no more after that, until he woke to find the villagers standing around his bed with worried frowns on their faces.

How did these ascetic monk-like entities vanish him in front of the villager's eyes? Who are they?

~~~~

A Romanian researcher, Mrs Caprarescu, had an interview with a man called 'E.H.' who claims he had an astonishing experience in the Piatra Mare Seven Stairs Mountains of Romania.

Seven Stairs Canyon lies in the middle-western part of Piatra Mare Mountains. The Romanian authorities posted a notice at the entrance of the canyon warning hikers not to enter and to choose a detour away from this route. However, many hikers and tourists choose to take the stairs that climb so close to the rocks and waterfalls, with spectacular views of the gorges. It is literally a wooden and metal staircase. The water from the seven waterfalls can make the steps a little slippery.

Says traveller Corina Chirileasea, 'My third attempt to climb the ladders pinned to the rock was successful this summer. My first attempt, I was in my early 20's, had no fears and lots of energy, so I crossed the canyon like a breeze. The second attempt however, a couple of years ago, was unsuccessful – the ladders were shaky and the whole experience was terrifying – I chose to return after climbing only a few stairs of the ladder.'

Says booking company viator.com, who organize trips to the stairs says; 'Visit the dramatic beauty of Canionul Sapte Scari (Seven Ladders Canyon). 'Choose between two hiking routes that pass through woods and meadows and climb vertical ladders and cross suspended bridges inside the canyon. After a scenic hike through meadows and forests, descend into the canyon to gain incredible views of waterfalls and ancient rock formations and explore under the guidance of a professional instructor. Ideal for lovers of adventure and adrenaline junkies.'

Well, the Romanian researcher Mrs. Caprarescu's interview with Mr. E.H. has been translated; Source: http://www.thelivingmoon.com/46ats_members/Lisa20 12/03files/Bucegi_Mountains_The_Mystery.html
And he says that within the Canionul Sapte Scari (Seven Ladders Canyon), he discovered something very strange;'In the Carpathians there is a gateway to another universe. Mr E.H. is not a "paranormal" person or mysterious in behaviour or appearance. He is an Ex engineer, divorced with no children, who retired in 1988 and was then able to fully devote to his passion: which was hiking.'

'We were asked to protect his name. His life changed for him one autumn day in 1990. His story is as follows: "It was 11 a.m. on 22nd September, 1990. I was on one of my routes on the Great Piatra Seven Stairs. The day was warm even in the shadow of the forest. I had about a half-hour to the hut, and slowed down to enjoy the beauty of the landscape. I started getting lost intentionally, to change the trail monotony. My trail climbed to a peak and I saw something bizarre, like a spark to my right, the sun reflecting on an object. I immediately thought that it came from cans or jars left in the forest.'

'A curiosity pulled me over to it. I first saw it at about 30 meters height, and I began to climb, but then I saw nothing, as I was at a different angle to the sun. After a few minutes of climbing, I began to ask myself questions; I was in a clearing, and was quite visible, but I did not see any object capable of reflecting light. I was about to continue when I saw something I find it hard to describe.'

'It was an elliptical vertical shape. The landscape was deformed, moving, as would be seen through a curved glass. It was behind a tree; the rear part of the tree trunk was deformed, elliptical, veiled. It resembled a perspective that you see through gasoline vapor.'

'I approached and with astonishment, I realized that I did not see any material object there that could generate such an effect; there was nothing there. The Ellipse was about 1 meter in diameter and 20 metres high, floating. It was transparent; except the wave, the fog behind it.'

'The edges were smooth, and the phenomenon of the optic ended abruptly. What could i do? I thought, trying to convince myself that I had in front of me a natural phenomenon, which obviously, it was not. I spent a few moments looking around it and then tried to touch it.'

'Fortunately, an instinct for fear made me take hold of a fallen tree branch. The first time I touched the edges of the ellipse it had elastic resistance, as if I have clicked on a balloon.'

'When I moved the branch into the ellipse center, I did not encounter any resistance; it went in smoothly, but the branch became invisible! It was like a hole and the branch was totally gone, and i continued to see the scenery behind it. The branch was about 50 inches long. When I drew it out, I saw with horror that it was no longer than 50 inches long! Part of it had completely disappeared! The end was severed, as if by a high precision saw. Then I thought; what would have happened if it were my hand instead of the branch!'

'I repeated the procedure again, with other tree branches. Then I tied a stone with rope and threw it in – the result was the same each time! Anything that went into that form did not come back. In this moment I was scared. It was getting too late and I decided to go. Before I left, I marked all the trees around me with a knife.'

'After a hot soup, I told the chalet supervisor all that had happened. The man knew me, so he did not think me crazy. He said he'd never seen anything like that in the woods, but anything is possible and that he would not be surprised if it contained "a new army technology."

At evening meal, I was approached by the son of the chalet supervisor, 12 year old Stephen, who I knew quite well too.

"I heard you speak with my dad," he said. "You know, I saw the ghost of the woods."

'I started to listen to him and learned that he had been with two shepherds when he saw the first ellipse. He had returned again several times to that place. I learned everything from him; about its shape and its two phases: when it looks transparent, which was the state in which I saw it, it allows objects entry. When seen in its other condition, as the boy had seen it, it is larger and white and it is then 'closed.' It works in reverse then, and it is closed to us on our side, but it lets the other side objects pass through it.'

'I returned two weeks later. I took the boy and we went to the place. Arriving in the clearing, our disappointment was enormous: there was no ellipse. It had disappeared. The trees I had marked gave me confidence we were definitely in the right place. But it was gone.'

'Throughout the winter, I gradually took the forest out of my mind. Then, a friend I'd told this story to, came to visit. He was very agitated and showed me a German magazine that had an article similar to the phenomena I'd seen, and it mentioned an organization that studies these strange ellipses, called Open Doors Research Group'.

'I wrote to them and received information back from them. It assured me that forms such as the one I'd seen have appeared from time immemorial and are even described in many old texts.'

'Just one example in more recent times they gave as a Mr. B. Roscott, a British man who was an engineer. He apparently saw a gate in 1962 when he was out walking in Manchester, England. He saw it for a period of two months during which time it appeared to remain open. In fact, it was this experience which led to the founding of the Open Doors Research Group, for the purpose of recording and observing 'doors' all over the world. They have recorded more than 230 'doors' so far, from as far a field as Russia, the U.S. and Europe.'

'This research group,' says Mr. E.H., state that the 'doors' or 'gates' usually remain open for eight weeks in every year. The larger they are, the correlation is that the longer they are likely to remain open. Circular gates have been recorded too.'

A 'gate' they say, passes through four distinct phases: 'Initiation, Access status, Power status and Closing.' Phases 2 and 3 do not occur necessarily in that order. No one has been able so far to open a gate or close it. All we know, from observations in the field, is that these openings have very intense radiation, which can be harmful to biological organisms. When the door is open for our world, we can insert any object or being into it, but nothing comes from the other side. In this state, it is transparent, showing only the optical phenomena.'

When it has closed, 'at this stage, a gate is whitish in colour, does not allow access from us, but operates as an open-door for the other side. It can bring objects (and beings?), which are always described as white ball-shaped moving with great speed, rolling on the ground or a short height.' This, from their observations, are the things that come out of it, from 'the other side.'

What else might come through it, from the other side, that they have not observed? Or do these white-ish ball-shaped fast-moving objects take on a new form and manifest into something else? Into beings? Entities? Monsters?

If the pieces of wood disappeared when Mr E.H. put them into the ellipse, would his arm have disappeared too, if he had put it in? Or his whole body, if he had walked into it? What if he had stumbled into it, without having noticed it by chance?

He for one, certainly believed that this was an obvious possibility, and fortunately for him, he resisted the temptation to put any part of himself inside of it.

Where did the pieces of wood, that were severed and 'taken' go? Could a person literally walk unknowingly through one of these circles or gates, and simply never come back out? Could they literally be 'disappeared'? Into another dimension? Into another world? And never return? – like the tree branch which came back, much shorter and somehow severed as though by some sharp instrument? What severed it?

What did the Chalet supervisor mean about "a new army technology?" What did he mean 'severed, as if by a high precision saw'? What then could this then do to a human being, who happened to walk into one, with no warning and no knowledge...?

Outside the New Age Mecca of Sedona, where it's already believed there is a vortex or portals to other worlds, lies a ranch that is infamous for visitors that do not seem to belong in our world. Sedona itself is located in the middle of Arizona, at an elevation of 4500 feet and set within large red-rock canyons and mountains.

Outside of Sedona, down a long dirt road which trails through the desert, you come to a deserted ranch. It is not advised that visitors go there however; it is strictly forbidden to trespass on that land. The land now belongs to the US government, or rather it is the property of the U.S. Forest Service. There are hiking trails that lead you to the ranch, but signs warn you not to enter.

The Ranch was purchased by Bob Bradshaw back in 1960. He was a photographer and an actor, who had moved to Oak Creek Canyon in the 1940's. He'd opened a photography store and when Hollywood began using the desert scenery for their Westerns, he was much in demand. The plot of land he purchased in 1960 is 140 acres with an old house situated on the land. He put the land to good use, establishing it as a location for filming both movies and commercials. Later, it was developed by his son as a destination for jeep tours and horseback riding.

Whether strange things had been happening there before or not, in the early 1990's he, along with his wife Linda and their sons began to record the disturbances they experienced there, and these disturbances were far from usual. By 1995 they had published a book with the help of researcher Tom Dongo, packed with descriptions of their strange encounters, along with highly anomalous photographs.

It began at first with strange lights appearing in the normally clear desert sky;
'Perhaps it may appear a bit far-fetched to some, and for this I will not apologise,' says Linda Bradshaw. 'What is, is. The night-time comes. There is often a feeling of a "presence," not completely discernible yet just enough to put a person on alert. The sounds come and our dogs bark frantically. At other times these same

dogs cower in a corner and whimper.'

It began with meteor showers. 'Several lights shot directly sideways rather than down, and they had a different intensity.' Curious about this, she decided to drive up to the highest point of the nearby ridge overlooking the canyon the following evening; a canyon, she says, 'rumoured to hide a secret military base. This information only heightened my curiosity.'

While there, she saw 'Some sort of airborne vehicle with flashing red lights. There was no sound. It began a quick descent. I waited for the craft to rise again – it did not.' White streaks of light split off from the craft as it began its descent.

Then hovering, just behind her truck, she saw a large ball of white, diming and then brightening repeatedly. Inside it was a small glowing ball. 'The pulse it emitted had the same cadence as a heartbeat. I instantly perceived an intelligence about it. There was no question in my mind – this was a life form of some sort.'

'It is common to walk around the ranch and spot small pinpoints of light blinking off and on' in the trees and bushes. 'Who or what are they?'

Almost always, if she takes a photo of these lights, nothing appears on her camera film, although chillingly in one photo however, 'in the sky a craft appears to be flying and in the lower left corner there is what I first thought to be a bush or tree. On closer scrutiny it has the appearance of a humanoid, possibly carrying something in its arms.'

One night, while wandering outside with her camera, 'I found that I was in the centre of a white fog-like mist,' but there had been no fog that evening. 'There was no physical sensation – no cold or wet to this fog-like mass, but I instantly knew that I must get out of the fog, which is exactly what I did.'

This incident she describes makes me wonder, do the people who go missing find themselves suddenly enveloped in a mist or fog?

Another time, 'There before me appeared a huge and brilliant light in the sky. It was as if someone had turned on a giant TV in the dark. It remained there for only a few seconds.'

Again, this gives pause for thought; could a person be whisked away, taken into the bright light and 'disappeared' when the light goes off?

Perhaps the most disturbing is the encounter she had with the 'invisible' thing. One evening, her dogs were barking frantically at something, something that was invisible. 'I became instantly nauseous. Something my height hissed loudly in my face. I was alone out there with this 'thing.' I demanded the creature be gone in the name of my Father and myself as a child of God.'

'As quick as the words left my mouth I heard a small pop in the air and the entity was gone. I would like to say I pulled myself together, but my heart pounded. It is a good idea not to play games with these beings. They don't have to obey someone who is uncertain of their own spiritual allegiance.'

What would someone do, with no dogs to warn them, out all alone and without the innate confidence to warn the entity off with words of faith?

Even more oddities are said to have happened at the isolated ranch including bigfoot, grays and reptilian encounters and even sightings of dinosaurs; that was until 2003, when it was purchased by the U.S. Government, for up to 20 years 'to conduct long-term climate change research at the site.'

What do we make of some of these strange encounters and incidents? Is this Inter-dimensional evidence? (For more, read 'Merging Dimensions' by Tom Dongo.)

Could there really be some kind of secret military base close-by? Justin Trimble, President of C.U.N.B.D. (Citizens for U.N. Base Disclosure) wrote back in 1998 about his concerns and describes talking with the ranch owner then.

'I called Mr. Bradshaw. He says that there certainly have been some unusual activities. He explains that a few years back, the military were involved in a large operation to build "tunnels" through Sycamore Canyon and Secret Canyon. He said that when they were building these tunnels, the water troughs on his ranch would vibrate violently. He's seen large buses with 'U.N.' painted on them, with tinted windows. They drive by his house. He says the U.S. Forest Service and local media are not allowed to talk about these military operations, but they know about them.'

'His son John has had run-ins with these supposed "U.N." officials. One threatened to pull a gun on him after he demanded to see credentials. Our own findings are of black helicopters, convoys of military vehicles near Secret Mountain, and confrontations with armed military guards.'

'We have a strong feeling that for one to understand and comprehend what is happening, it is not something meant to be known by the public and is taking place underground. It is worth noting that the areas spoken of are designated Forest Service Wilderness areas that are not known to have any military affiliation. They are also extremely remote areas.'

From an anonymous, email 1/6/98; "Were you here when those bodies, (beheaded), were found out in Long/Boynton Canyon area? A friend of mine was parked next to the van of one of the women and was talking to her just hours before she and the other two were apparently killed."

"Another friend of mine was called in on the investigation to help determine whether or not it was ritual murder. Red Rock News refused to print anything about it for at least 2 weeks and I never did find out if they covered it at all. Most of the official voices of Sedona denied the 'rumors'."

Chapter Twelve

Isle of Mull Disappearance

It's an unexplained mystery that no-one has been able to solve. It's a mystery that has puzzled, perplexed and baffled both experts and amateur sleuths combined, ever since it happened.

A man's body is found up on a hill, four months after he disappeared on the Isle of Mull. He was last seen getting into his private plane. His body was found with only a tiny scratch, but it hadn't been where it was found when all the search parties had looked for him, repeatedly.

Then it was found in the exact spot where searchers had looked, many, many times. What on earth happened to Peter Gibbs? And how did he get to where he was found?

The man in question was Norman Peter Gibbs, known as Peter. He was a talented violinist in the 1950's, 60's, and '70's, and he'd been Head of BBC Northern Ireland Symphony Orchestra as well as BBC Scotland's Orchestra leader. He'd been a fighter pilot in World War II with 41 Squadron RAF, from January 1944 to March 1945. It was said that after the War, he had his Tiger Moth plane modified so that he could fit his violin into the baggage compartment.

His comrades in the RAF called him 'a daredevil,' and a plain talking man, while those who knew him from the orchestra described him as a practical joker, such as the time he once flew over a live Orchestra performance and 'bombed' them all with bags of flour.

While playing for the Philharmonic orchestra in Washington D.C., he stood up to chastise the German conductor, who it was believed had joined the Nazi party during the War, although no doubt he had no choice in this matter. Gibbs chastised the conductor in front of the rest of the orchestra for his arrogance and rudeness, which Gibbs had not been alone in noticing.

The conductor, in response, demanded an apology and refused to perform again until Gibbs was sacked. The orchestra refused to back the German conductor however, and Gibbs played on for the rest of the tour, while the German and his lawyers left to take up a new position at the Berlin and Vienna Philharmonics orchestras.

The man whose body was later to be inexplicably found on the Isle of Mull up a hill, went on to form the 'Peter Gibbs quartet,' which, according to musician David Myers, was a rather Avant guarde affair. One of the violinists in his Quartet was another man called Carter, who was reported as saying, "Being made up of very talented young musicians it was immediately successful, but Gibbs being Gibbs, he demanded such high standards of them that it inevitably disbanded.

Gibbs insisted that each member should sit in different corners of the room with their backs to each other and start (playing) by some sort of intuition! This and many other crazy ideas proved too much for the others who all left."

According to Mr. Peter Mountain, who played in the London Symphony Orchestra with Gibbs, he heard of the time that Gibbs was getting a lift to the orchestra performance with another member, Rodney Friend, but they got caught up in traffic that had ground to a halt at Hyde Park Corner in the centre of London, in the middle of rush hour. They would be late to their performance at the Royal Albert Hall if the traffic did not shift, and so rather than resigning themselves to this fate, Gibbs asked to sit in the driver's seat.

They swopped seats and Gibbs took hold of the wheel. He crossed over into the oncoming traffic lane, shot into Hyde Park, came out the other end, shot through red traffic lights, and "nonchalantly parked outside the Artists entrance!" It would seem then, that Gibbs was a man full of zest, a spirit of adventure and much daring.

During his time in the Orchestras, he had also been flying privately. In 1957, he had joined the Surrey Flying Club, and he'd been flying private airplanes ever since. He owned a De Havilland Tiger Moth.

Not only was Gibbs a fearless daredevil, but he was ambitious too. While still head of BBC Scotland's Orchestra, he began to make money as a property developer. In 1975, he finally left his professional musician's career and began to expand his property development business.

He was doing very well and making good money and had great plans. One of these plans was a little unusual, although not unique. He wanted to buy a hotel and have a private landing strip, so that wealthy guests could arrive by private jet.

On Christmas Eve of 1975, he returned to Scotland where he had lived while in the orchestra there. He was accompanied by his girlfriend Felicity Grainger. It would be his birthday the following day, Christmas Day. He planned to stay on the Isle of Mull to celebrate. The Isle of Mull is a small island of the Inner Hebrides and lies off the west coast of Scotland. It is comprised of just 337.97 square miles, with a tiny population of under 3,000.

Gibbs flew himself and Felicity to the Island in his private plane, landing on the small airstrip not far from the hotel The Glenforsa, where they had booked to stay. A small number of hotels in the US and the Bahamas did have a landing strip, as he envisaged building, but so too did this hotel, although the private landing strip was only allowed to be used in daylight hours, as it had no lights.

It also did not have all the usual accompaniments such as traffic control, and radar. For this reason, the hotel only gave permission to land during fair weather and daylight, in the spring and summer months.

Glenforsa airfield is located on the north coast of the Island. According to Glenforsa Airfield Ltd, "The runway is a grass strip 780 metres by 28 metres. The length is level, but the width has a slight slope down to the sea. Livestock may be on the airstrip from October to April, and Geese may present a hazard throughout the year. Turbulence can be expected on approaches with strong southerly winds. If using Runway 07, fly a curved approach from base leg inside the hill. Approach - Due to high local terrain you will not be able to make ground contact until visual with the airfield." This will become important later...

The hotel itself is a14-room Norwegian wooden log hotel, imported from Norway. They say "it is situated on the sheltered East coast of Mull at the narrow waist of the Island, making it a great base to explore. Outdoor pursuits include angling, bird watching and hill walking. It is an ancient landscape with many standing stones and cairns. Operated by the Hotel is Mull's only airfield which sits between the Hotel and the Sound of Mull. Direct to the Hotel, Glenforsa is adjacent to a well-maintained grass airstrip." Again, this is important for later reference.

Gibbs and his girlfriend flew from North Connel airfield, near Oban, in western Scotland, where Gibbs had hired a two-seater Cessna 150H light aircraft, registration G-AVTN, equipped with navigation and communication equipment, but not equipped with parachutes. This was normal - it would have been very unusual for parachutes to be carried in any model of the modern light aircrafts.

The journey from Oban airfield to the private landing strip next to the Hotel on the Island of Mull took around ten minutes. On the night of the 23rd December they were booked in to stay at the Glenforsa hotel. On the morning of 24th, Christmas Eve, he flew Felicity to the Isle of Skye with him, where they checked out a few of the hotels, in view of his property development plans. On the afternoon of the 24th he flew them back to the Isle of Mull, landing just before 4 pm, just as it was beginning to get dark. So far, all was well.

They ate in the hotel restaurant that evening, during which they shared a bottle of red wine, and some reports say whiskey too. By all accounts, from the hotel staff, Gibbs was in a great mood that evening, although he did express disappointment that it seemed he would not be able to fly on his birthday, Christmas Day, as a storm was due to come in.

At around 9 pm, when they were still in the hotel restaurant, he apparently suddenly decided he would fly tonight instead. He had a plan – he wanted to see if it was possible to land on the hotel airstrip in the dark.

He quickly left his chair and returned to his room where he changed into his flying gear, then returned to the dining room and requested his girlfriend come outside with him, armed with two torches to use as make-shift landing lights to guide him home. He asked her to follow him outside and wait on the landing strip for him, with the two torches placed on either side of the landing strip to show him where the landing strip was in the dark.

As hotel staff overheard his plans, they offered their opinion on this folly and strongly tried to persuade him against this rash plan – it was not allowed and of course, they could immediately see the danger in this experiment. Gibbs responded by chastising them, telling them that he was not asking for their permission – merely informing them of his decision.

He explained to them briefly that he was a highly competent and experienced pilot, and there was no risk because his girlfriend Miss Grainger would be guiding him back inland with the torch lights. This would then prove to him whether he would be able to go ahead with the plan for buying a hotel himself and having a landing strip put in, that could be used day or night.

He'd been a fighter pilot in the Royal Air Force in World War II, so this quick night-time flight was hardly going to faze him, presumably. Besides which, the flight would be over and done with in the space of a few minutes.

So, he went ahead, going out to his small plane and starting it up. Felicity sat in the plane with him as it taxied along the landing strip and then he stopped to let her out. Presumably, he didn't need too much of a run-up to take off.

As he took to the sky in his plane, his girlfriend/assistant duly placed the two lit torches at the end of the grass landing strip, pointing out toward the sea. Then there she stood, by the landing strip, in the cold and the wind, awaiting his return.

She waited for an hour. He should have returned within five minutes or so. He never returned.

Despite an ensuing huge air, sea and land search, no trace of him nor his plane were found. Of course, the most logical explanation was that he tragically, for some reason, crashed his plane into the sea. Perhaps it had engine failure, or it was pilot error of some kind, and terribly sadly, the pilot and his plane sunk into the depths of the ocean. This would completely explain why he was not found – he was now lying dead at the bottom of the sea.

The Island itself was searched, in case they were wrong, but no sign of him or his plane were found, despite the police and hundreds of volunteers searching the remote barren and isolated land below his flight path, and the RAF and Navy Air Service helicopters scouring the island for any sign of the plane wreck.

However, this was not the end to the story – it really is just the beginning, and yet the end is also cryptically unfinished. You see, four months after that fateful night on Christmas eve, in April 1975 a shepherd called Donald MacKinnon stumbled across Gibb's dead body. It was lying on a hillside overlooking the sound of Mull and Pennygown Cemetery, less than a mile from the grass airstrip from which Gibbs had taken off.

He was lying on his back across a log. The owner of the hotel, David Howitt saw the body in-situ and he immediately confirmed that the body was wearing the clothes and flying boots that Peter Gibbs had been wearing on the evening he disappeared. It looked as though he had simply lain down there and died.

He was entirely alone – there was no plane wreckage around him. His body was pristine save for a tiny cut on his leg. He did not look at all like a victim of a catastrophic plane crash. He did not look like someone who had plummeted to the land from a plane, nor crashed into the sea, escaped from his plane wreck in the icy winter waters of the sea, swum inland and climbed his way onto land, then succumbed to his injuries and died.

His body was taken away for medical examination by Dr W.D.S. McLay, chief medical Officer of Strathclyde Police and his death was ruled by the coroner as having been caused by "exposure." After his body was discovered on land, search parties went out again across the island, dragging the inland lochs and searching through woods for the plane wreckage again. But no plane wreckage was found.

Was it at all possible he had swum ashore, in temperatures as low as 6 degrees centigrade, where the life-expectancy for survival in the water was given as under an hour. It would seem, even for a former World War II fighter pilot, to have been a feat of superhuman endeavour, although his son says he was shot down four times by the Germans during World War II.

His son said what he did that night, attempting to fly inland with no navigation and no proper landing strip lights, was quite in keeping with his father's personality. What's perhaps most pertinent here though is that in order for him to have got to the hill where he was found, he would have had to cross over the road which led directly to the hotel.

Surely, wouldn't he have headed along the road with the intention of reaching warmth and shelter rather than climb a hill? If he had the astonishing ability to climb free of his watery grave and make it back to shore intact, why would he cross the road and climb 400ft up a hill to die of hypothermia and exposure, when all he had to do was to follow that road back to the Hotel?

Gibb's son, Alan is not convinced his father swam to shore and climbed up to his death. When speaking to the BBC he said that he 'recreated' the route his Father took that night, up the hill. "There's almost a continuous vertical wall of rock; some of it is two metres high, some of it's three metres high, and relatively few gaps. Now this is the climb that I attempted in the company of my husky, who's pretty eager and pulls pretty hard."

"In about 40 minutes, I got half-way to where the body

was found. There were points where I had to turn around and go back. It was boggy. I could not make it myself, in daylight. I would stake my every bit of my reputation that nobody swam directly to shore and climbed up that hill in the dark."

If he had been climbing vertically on rocks, in the dark, with heavy wet boots and jacket, how could he have no scratches or bumps or marks on his body?

Even more astonishing was, how could his body not have been discovered in all the searches, after his plane disappeared? How could the searchers have possibly missed his body, when the very spot at which he was found, was covered multiple times by search parties?

The coroner said that his body was "Entirely consistent with lying there for a period of four months," which was the amount of time between him disappearing that night and being found on the steep hill, and yet, what is very odd is that he had no sea salt on his body; surely that would be completely impossible, given that he had apparently, presumably swum back to shore.

The explanation given as to why his body had no sea salt on it, was that he had been lain there so long that the elements had removed all trace. And yet, surely, wind and gusts there on that tiny remote island, surrounded by the sea, would be full of sea salt, as the breezes swirled around in the elements?

Forensic tests on his body detected no marine organisms at all, neither on his body or his clothes or the boots he still wore. No matter how heavy the rain might have been in the four months he was supposed to have been lying there, it seems highly unlikely that no traces of the sea would be on him after his swim back to shore, particularly for example inside his boots, which would have been saturated with sea water had he swam ashore.

Then there is the inexplicable condition of his body. It was entirely intact, with no injuries whatsoever save for a tiny scratch on his leg. His plane was still missing, and so no other conclusion could be given that it had crashed, and as the entire island had been searched for its wreckage, it had to have presumably crashed into the sea, but a crash surely would have caused him injuries? And indeed, surely, he would have been in a frantic and desperate struggle to eject himself from the plane while underwater, and that would seem impossible to do without causing more than a tiny scratch to himself. He would have fought with all his might to free himself from the plane wreck as it sunk to the depths.

No-one could really wrap their heads around any of this. Then, in September 1986, almost a decade after Gibb's body had been found, two brothers, Richard and John Grieve were clam diving in the Sound of Mull, when they discovered, at a depth of 100 feet, a wreckage. This was about a mile to the east of the direct approach to the grass landing strip.

When the wreckage was inspected, it appeared to have crashed with some impact. The engine had been detached from the airframe and was some distance from it. One of the wheels was missing. The wings were detached and lying at some distance away from the body of the plane. The front Perspex screen was shattered. Both doors were still locked. Escape could only have been achieved through the shattered Perspex screen and this would have to have been achieved by climbing over and through sharp jagged edges of Perspex. This would have been difficult to achieve without some injury to the body, one would think.

However, for some reason, the plane was not actually recovered, and the photos the clam brothers had taken of the wreckage were not good enough to allow expert air-accident inspectors to assess whether the crash had been survivable.

Local man, Richard Grieve, when talking to Ian Punnit of the BBC in their investigation of the strange tale, said he found it implausible to believe that Gibbs swam back to shore. He said he himself uses an 8mm thick dry suit whenever he enters the icy waters. When the plane was found, the doors were locked. He also can't explain why that would be. "I think if he knew he was going to crash, and he must have had some warning, he would have had at least a door open he could have got out of, unless he was committing suicide. I wouldn't like to swim in that even in my dry-suit."

"When he got ashore, why would he cross a road and walk up a steep hill; it just doesn't make sense. I just don't see that what came up in the official reports could be true. I was talking to some farmers and on the night of the crash they said they heard a plane go up over their farm. There was some talk about him going to Northern Ireland, something to do with the IRA – that would have taken about an hour, hour and a half. You'd have thought the authorities, for all it would have taken to lift the plane, all you would need is a couple of airbags. I doubt the official story – there's too many things that don't ring true. The more I think of it, the more I doubt it."

It is perplexing to think that surely, the plane should have been lifted out of the water and inspected; but the Air Safety Board never got that chance. Why would that be?

Ian Punnet turned to retired engineering academic Alan Organ, who has dedicated many years to looking into this mystery. He said it was simply impossible to jump from anything higher than 10 feet without very serious injury or death.

(for more please see https://mysteryinksite.wordpress.com/2016/03/01/the-mull-air-mystery/ and https://www.bbc.co.uk/programmes/b066fqcr)

After his body had been found on the hill, a fatal accident enquiry had been held on the mainland, in Oban on 24th June 1976 (without the plane). The enquiry, and the following media coverage seemed only to raise even more anomalies. The local shepherd who had stumbled across Gibb's body was very forthright in stating that he and his sheepdog had walked past the spot where the body was discovered, on multiple occasions after Gibbs had disappeared, and he had never seen the body there in all that time.

He insisted – the man's body was not there. This was backed-up by Mountain Rescue teams who had also searched the exact area several times and seen no body there, as well as all the volunteers. In fact, most of the inhabitants of the tiny Island were extremely surprised that he was found in that spot, after so many volunteers had covered the area searching for him.

They also expressed surprise that his body was completely intact. They knew, from past experience, being very familiar with the land there and its environment, that bodies left out in the wild Scottish Highlands and Islands, whether human or animal, stood a very slim chance of not being picked at by natural predators. Very strangely, this was not the case for Gibb's body. It had suffered no predation, and this, they felt, was extremely odd, given that it was supposed to have been lying there for four months.

David Howitt, for Mull historical and archaeological society, says, "In my experience as a farmer, any corpses lying around, whether cattle, sheep, or deer, are soon attacked by scavengers and reduced to piles of bones." He adds, "A shepherd, Robert Duncan, told me that he had been past that place several times with his dogs in the intervening period and found nothing. Also, there had been a huge land/air search of the area in the days following the disappearance, which also drew a blank."

Cryptically he says, "One wonders how much experience the pathologists had of bodies exposed for such periods. Supposing they had reported that its condition was not consistent with this period of exposure, what would the repercussions have been? Best to give the expected answer and allow the whole tragic affair to be quietly forgotten..."

Speculation and rumour was that his body could have been dumped there, at some time after his death, despite the medical examiner's ruling. Some of the suggested explanations put forth after the discovery of his body were that he had been on a clandestine mission for MI6 in Northern Ireland. He had worked and lived in Ireland while playing the Violin for BBC Ireland Orchestra, and of course, he had been in the Air Force during the war.

'The troubles' in Northern Ireland were ongoing, and so this speculative theory was that the IRA had captured him then returned him to the Island after killing him, to leave a calling card, as such, and to taunt the powers that be that the IRA would not be messed with, although this would seem quite a complicated and extreme theory.

Perhaps he was smuggling something precious and illicit? And yet, there was never any suggestion that Gibbs was anything more than a Patriot who had fought for his country's freedom and an honest business man, so it would seem very improbable that he was up to no good. But had he been trying to fake his own death and it went horribly wrong? Or had it been some kind of insurance scam gone wrong? And yet, if so, why would he end up on a log on a hill with four months of time missing between his disappearance and subsequent discovery. There was also nothing in his business life that suggested anything other than an honest and successful man.

Did he have another, secret reason to attempt what most pilots would say was a lunatic attempt to land in the dark, other than to see if it could be done? After all, if it could be done, surely he would still have been hard pressed to find other private charter pilots willing to gamble their lives on seeing if they too could land in the dark on a tiny airstrip, all for the purpose of staying at a hotel? Why would any other pilots be willing to possibly and quite probably crash and die by booking a stay in a hotel that required night-time landing on a grass landing strip modelled without lights?

The purpose of Gibb's planned idea was for luxury guests to come to a hotel he would purchase, not suicidal private charter pilots or passengers. It was later discovered that when Gibbs hired his private plane, his license had actually expired, although he did have over 2,000 hours of flying experience. According to the research of David Byers, former Chief Producer of Music & Arts for the BBC, on one occasion, and it was to be only once for good reason, business man Morrison Dunbar and Stradivarius violin owner (Stradivarius violins being the most expensive instruments in the world) was invited by Gibbs to fly from Glasgow airport over Loch Lomond and the Trossachs National Park in the Highlands of Scotland.

Said Morrison Dunbar afterwards; "It immediately became clear that Peter was navigating solely by means of a small AA Handbook." (In other words, he was navigating his plane by using an Automobile Association road map!) "When he got lost, he would fly down and take a quick look at the road signs!" Gibbs was no doubt a true daredevil, but what has never been solved is the mystery of how his body ended up where it did.

Curiously, it was alleged that when Gibbs never returned that night and while his girlfriend Felicity was awaiting the arrival of the police, she mentioned that he had told her; "If everything went wrong, he would throttle back and jump to safety."

Well, again, jumping on land would have, no matter how low, resulted in some form of injuries to his body, and the plane did not land on the island, and the belief that he somehow managed to swim in the freezing water with both his heavy flying boots and heavy jacket, would seem an impossible feat.

Why would an experienced albeit dare-devil pilot even

want to have to jump out of a plane in the pitch black on a winter's night, not even knowing if he were jumping into the sea or jumping onto land; either of which could only have spelt certain disaster and most probable death. He certainly did not come across as a man who had an overriding death-wish.

No matter the practical joker that he was, he had great future plans in business, was a man of ambition and had made a great success of his life. He certainly never indicated to anyone who knew him that he wouldn't mind killing himself. Yet he must have known how dangerous it was to do what he was planning, so was there some other reason for it? What could that reason have possibly been? He knew he had no parachute in the aircraft.

Curiously, the owners of the hotel, David and Pauline Howitt claimed that, while watching Gibbs manoeuvring his plane before take-off, they had both seen two torches being moved separately at the end of the runway.

This seemed to imply the presence of a third person on the runway, although Gibb's girlfriend Felicity maintained that only she handled both torches. Had it really been Gibbs at the controls that night some people wondered? Or had he planned his disappearance to escape a personal problem or business debts? And yet if he had planned to run-away from it all and start a new life, how did he end up dead up a steep hill four months after his plane vanished?

One pilot says, "Several aspects to this story have my spidey sense tingling. The plane comes with locking mechanisms to prevent accidental opening in flight, but they are capable of being opened from inside of the aircraft. Barring some extreme damage to the doors that somehow warped them in a way they could not be opened (Unlikely), there would be no reason for a pilot to choose to escape through the window.

If these divers found the locks were still in place when they discovered the aircraft, it suggests something quite different than the pilot was incapable of leaving via the doors.' Does he mean sabotage and subterfusion of some kind? (This would apply presumably for the theory that Gibbs disembarked from the plane in air, when he realized something was wrong, rather than under the water.)

Let's just pretend that rather than try to do a controlled landing (much safer according to experienced pilots and air experts) he really did jump out of the plane mid-air, and by some miraculous divine intervention he didn't get injured, in any way, which simply seems impossible, but still, if we pretend this did happen, how did he magically appear 6 weeks later, dead, lying across a log in a spot that had already been searched passed, numerous times?

Had someone got in the plane, hijacked it, held him hostage, and somehow, he ends up dead on a hill having been kept somewhere else for four months? And yet, his girlfriend had taxied with him in the plane before he took off.

A mystery passenger would have to have got in after she got out, and yet the owners of the hotel, other staff and several guests had told reporters that they had watched him that night through the windows of the hotel, and no-one else could have been in the plane if his girlfriend had got in to taxi to the end of the grass landing strip, as the plane was just a two-seater. And, if he had been killed by a captor or captors, why not dispose of his body someone secret, where it would never be found, rather than put it somewhere in plain sight?

Steve Punt from the BBC asked the former owner, who was in charge of the airstrip that night, what he saw. "I came straight out with binoculars, and we said, "What on earth is that madman doing!" Before long, the plane disappears behind some trees, as is normal there, and they lost sight of its outbound trip, but as hotel guests learnt of the escapade, everyone rushed to the upstairs bar intending to watch his landing.

There were no lights on the landing strip to indicate to them exactly where the landing strip was and there was no visible moon that night, so in an attempt to improve their vision, the bar lights were turned off inside the hotel. David still has the two torches that were used that night at the end of the runway that night. They were tiny hand-held torches.

Some guests thought that Gibbs took an unusually long time to warm the engine of the plane up, while others said they were sure there were two people out on the end of the runway, as they believe they could see both torches moving at the same time, at a distance from one another. (Perhaps it does have to be added here that it was Christmas eve and people were there to celebrate the holiday season and no doubt, alcohol was being consumed that night.)

The former hotel owner added, in an aside, "My mother had her room of the hotel exorcised! Apparently, all sorts of nasty things happened in that room."

When the plane failed to return, hotel owner David drove his car down to the water and shone his headlights into the sea, attempting to see where the plane must have crashed. When showing the investigator where he had gone down to the water to look for Gibb's plane on the night he disappeared, they had to pass the cemetery to do so. "This old cemetery, its haunted rotten there," he said. "Time and again they've tried to put a roof on the Church, but the Fairies came each time and took it away."

Did Gibbs miraculously survive the crash completely uninjured, climb a steep hill in sodden heavy clothing and boots, (a hill his son failed to conquer in daylight) rather than go to the shelter of the hotel close-by, and then die from the elements, then someone took his body and hid it for a few months, then took it back, not being seen by anyone and leaving his body in pristine condition? That would seem like an impossible tale.

The owner of the hotel saw his body when it was found though and he says, "The only thing holding him together was his clothes – he was in a terrible state of decomposition.' So, this would shed doubt on the 'pristine' nature of his body. Interestingly, he also adds, "There was no question about it - he'd been walking down the hill."

The medical examiner did not see the body in situ. He received the body for post-mortem on the mainland. "He was clothed, and I just found this a very odd problem to be faced with. It's weird that the body didn't turn up fairly quickly after the crash; that's very unusual and one would expect fairly major injuries coming out of a plane like that. There was nothing to suggest he had come out of a plane flying at any speed at all. There was nothing to suggest he had died in one place and been taken and put in another place. There was a toxicology search for any poisons or medicines or alcohol and to the best of my recollection nothing was found by forensic scientists.

The result of the search for salt water was negative – it did not confirm the suggestion of salt water being present. The body was also tested for those little organisms that exist in the sea. This was negative. Lying exposed to rain water for four months I should imagine that much of the freshwater coming down from the sky, although this is not my specialism, but I would have thought it would have washed away any salt water present."

Yet surely his boots, which he was still wearing when his body was found, could not possibly have had no salt in them – unless, he had never been in the sea at all? And if he hadn't been in the sea, how did he escape from his plane uninjured and end up on the steep hill, then die?

"In the absence of anything else," said the medical examiner, "We were reduced to saying he had died simply of exposure and the consequence of loss of heat and loss of will to struggle, because where the body was, he was not far to the road."

Average survival time in this sea is 1 hour. He had an estimated 300 metres in the sea to swim, not the calm water of a swimming pool. 300 metres in a pool is not too bad. 300 metres in a winter sea, is another matter. It would have exhausted him, if he had made it. Why then would he start climbing a steep rock hill – unless he was trying to get his bearings?

But he would surely have known he had crossed a road – unless of course his feet had turned to jelly from the sheer exhaustion of trying to swim ashore in the wild freezing sea, still wearing heavy flying boots that would have become dead weights when waterlogged.

His brain, along with his feet would most probably have turned to jelly, numbness, fogginess, disorientation. Perhaps that was why he would not have noticed that he was crossing a road - his feet would not have had the ordinary ability to detect what he was walking on – they were feeling heavy and like jelly, and desensitized sufficiently to not be able to feel a tarmac surface.

After he crossed the road (which would have taken him straight to the shelter of the hotel) did he continue upwards, climbing rocks, because he did not know what direction he was heading in, and by getting higher he believed he would be able to pick up the lights of the hotel? And yet, he knew the rough layout of the small island, having flown there.

Yet, the medical examiner had said; "There was nothing to suggest he had come out of a plane flying at any speed at all."

The most curious aspect of this all is that where he was found, up the steep hill, was so hard to access, if he had climbed up out of the sea. As his son said, "In about 40 minutes, I got half-way to where the body was found. There were points where I had to turn around and go back. It was boggy. I could not make it myself, in daylight. I would stake my every bit of my reputation that nobody swam directly to shore and climbed up that hill in the dark."

And, how could his body not have been discovered there, in all the searches, after his plane disappeared? How could the searchers have possibly missed his body, when the very spot at which he was found, was covered multiple times by search parties?

What happened that Christmas eve night when Gibbs took off on his daredevil mission? What happened to his body in the four months between when he disappeared and when he was found?

Exactly how did he end up on that steep hill, dead?

Excerpt from Lured in the Woods:

Chapter 1: The Missing

On Sunday August 27th, 2017, hiker Rodney Letterman was hiking with his friend in Devil's Den State Park in Arkansas. He told his friend that he was not feeling well as they walked along the Butterfield Trail, and his friend later said that he offered to return to their car to fetch Mr Letterman's medication while Mr Letterman stayed where he was and waited for him to return. When the friend returned with the medication, Mr Letterman was no-where to be seen. All that remained of him was his cell phone, lying on the ground.

Parks Assistant Superintendent Tim Scott confirmed that the man's friend told them he went back to the car because Mr Letterman "felt fatigued and needed medication." When he returned to the trail, his partner was gone. Since then, no searchers and no hikers have come across any clues leading to Letterman's disappearance.

Parks Assistant Superintendent Scott, said that the densely wooded area and interconnecting trails were challenges that make it difficult to find people, however he added that the missing man had approximately a gallon and a half of water with him and temperatures had not been too hot or too cold, which was good for his chances of survival.

'Search Crews were working in shifts including through the night. Search and rescue teams have been using ATVs, horses and walking the trails on foot. They have searched close to 4,000 acres and six square miles,' he said.

Local News station NWA reported; 'The hunt continues for the man who lost his way on a popular Northwest Arkansas hiking trail. Outdoor enthusiasts are doing what they can to find the man lost in the wilderness. Hikers from all across the country are on the trail where 33-year-old Letterman was last seen. "They gave us a sheet and said this man had been missing for a week and so to keep our eyes out for him," hiker Brandon Roellig said.

NWA reported; 'One couple who've come from Fort Worth said they were on their toes now after hearing about the missing person.' Leighton Clark, one more of the many hikers said; "I don't know much but it just seems hard to believe that somebody could have just disappeared like that. We both looked a little bit and you know, didn't see anything. I didn't really want to see something in a way - Seeing a dead body isn't something most of us look forward to," Clark said.

'From Texas to Missouri, hikers are coming from all across the country. Park officials are informing everyone of their ongoing search and handing out flyers to every person on Butterfield Trail. The out of towners say what they've heard about the case is concerning.

Hiker Clark continued; "Considering they've been searching for so long, that they went out with dogs and horses, to not find somebody who presumably was close to the trail when he was left just seems really bizarre and makes you wonder what might've really happened."

On Thursday August 31st the search was scaled back and the command center moved to Devil's Den headquarters. The missing man's wife and family had arrived, but still no clues had been found that could shed light on where he had gone or where he was now.

On September 3rd; 'Searchers at Arkansas park remain hopeful missing hiker will be found alive,' reported the NWA Democrat Gazette. Assistant Superintendent at Devil's Den State Park Tim Scott again said; "We've covered those areas that were within the search areas pretty thoroughly and so we believe at this point it was a good reason to scale back the search."

Washington County Search and Rescue removed their command center from the park. All future search efforts would now run out of the visitor center. "We will look at maps, check where teams have been ... and make sure in that segmented map if there's areas that should be covered more extensively, we'll contact groups to go within that area."

127 searchers, dogs and horses covered almost 4,000 acres of the state park but with no luck. "Each search is

so different that it's hard to say what is normal and what is not ...it's based on a lot of things," says Scott. With Labor Day approaching, the park was likely to have 5,000 visitors over that weekend. "At the bulletin boards at the trailheads we've posted a photo, some information and who they can contact." He also said they would be handing out flyers to visitors hiking the Trail there. Still, despite the long search over days, and the number of hikers along the route he had taken, there was nothing to explain where he was and what had happened to him. He is still missing.

Adam Federman of the Adirondack Life wrote an excellent article back in 2010 on the numbers of people missing in the wilderness there. George LaForest disappeared in the woods. Described as an avid fisherman and a 3-4 pack-a-day smoker, he had gone to his familiar and usual spot to do some fishing. It was April 21st, 2006 and he was at Indian Lake, in the Adirondack Mountains, in the State of New York. Four days later he was reported missing by his wife, after he failed to arrive at work for an important scheduled meeting.

When the search for him began, his truck was located in the parking bay at Cedar River, a place popular with fishermen and swimmers alike. Inside his vehicle were worms for his fishing trip, his wallet and a number of personal items, but no clues to his disappearance. Forest Rangers, Fire-fighters and volunteers joined the search for him, all around the Indian Lake area. In fact, they covered a 25-square mile in their search for him, both sides of Cedar River. Kayakers and a dive team searched the water and K-9's helped the ground search. The search went on for several days.

State police said they believed the missing man could be carrying his rifles. They described him as an avid outdoorsman. Heavy rains had saturated the search area however, and this had washed away possible tracks and the five-day search found no clues at all about what had happened to the missing man nor where he could be.

Forest Ranger Lt. Steve Preston told reporter; "The rain washed out his tracks before we even started looking."

They pointed out that not even a cigarette butt was

found despite him being classified as a very heavy smoker and one would think that if he had been in the area for very long at all, he would have smoked a couple of cigarettes. This perhaps is the most important 'clue' – in that he surely could not have been in that location for very long before something happened to him which had caused him to disappear, somehow, without returning to his truck. Unless the rain had washed away the cigarette butts too – but then surely they would have still been somewhere in the vicinity?

After a search of eight continuous days, the official search was scaled back by the rangers and state police. 3775 man-hours had been logged in the search for him, on foot, on the water and in the air. His family, friends and co-workers were also all interviewed to see if any of them could shed light on his sudden unexpected vanishing.

"You could drive yourself crazy wondering what happened to him," his sister said. "I've tried to think of all the things that could have happened to him. Did he just walk away? Did he take his own life? Did someone take his life?" Although she says he was depressed after their father's death, she doesn't believe he would have committed suicide. "He told me there was no way he would leave his children."

The State police also found no evidence to make them believe he staged his disappearance. Just a handful of miles from where LaForest disappeared, 72-year-old Fred Gillingham also disappeared. On October 27th 2006, forest rangers called off their 12-day search for Mr Gillingham. He was a seasonal resident and had spent many summers alone at Indian Lake. He had last been seen in town buying supplies to close down his camp. He'd been reported missing on October 15th by a friend who was checking on him after he'd missed a dinner engagement the previous night. His car was found at a nearby trailhead but there was no sign of Mr Gillingham anywhere.

Just over two years later, in February 2009 according to the local newspaper the Enterprise, "Body discovered in woods tentatively identified as Gillingham." A hunter reported finding the remains of a person late in the afternoon in an area north of Rock River. The following morning rangers and the state police 'hiked in to the remote location and by Tuesday evening were trying to remove the body by foot and by boat.' "They're still working on getting the body out," state Department of Environmental Conservation spokesman Dave Winchell.

In between Fred Gillingham's disappearance and George LaForest's disappearance, Forest Ranger Tom Eakin noticed an unoccupied campsite on Cedar River Road near the trailhead of Lost Pond in Moose River Plains, amid a 35-square mile forest in the Adirondacks. When he returned to the same area, he saw the camp again and it looked to him as though it had lain undisturbed and uninhabited. This aroused his concern and so he reported it to his supervisor.

It was discovered that the camp belonged to a man called Jack Coloney, a 45-year-old amateur photographer. He'd signed into the Cedar River register on June 6th, 2009 and had indicated that his stay there would last one week and he would depart on the 14th June. It seems however, that he never left. Or if he did, he left everything behind, which would seem a strange thing to do. His kayak was still there by the river and personal belongings including his notebook were also still there.

Searchers teamed up to look for him, and the search was to last for ten days. The forest there was so dense that it made searching for him particularly gruelling. No one reported seeing him apart from the ranger when he registered his visit. After that, there were no witnesses to help shed light on what might have happened to him. It was an area where there would often be fishermen, but none of them had seen him.

DEC Forest Ranger Captain John Streif said the area is developing a reputation; 'Men have disappeared near Indian Lake leading some officials to nickname the area 'the Indian Lake Triangle.'

Its happened before this too though. On October 21, 1958 the Wellsville Daily Reporter covered the case of Howard Gilroy (né Leslie A. Wiggs) 'Reported missing October 10th after he failed to return from a climb of

4,261-foot Santanoni Peak in the Adirondacks. Search parties have combed the rugged mountain for him. But friends have told of seeing him in downtown Schenectady, where he had been employed as a clerk at the Army supply depot. He was laid off from the job and out of work since.' His friends must have been mistaken however, because thirty years later hikers uncovered his skeleton, a Kodak camera, and rusted thermos.

Harold T. Watkins 1958 book 'Mysteries Solved and Unsolved' relates the strange disappearance of a Dr. Thornton R. Sampson, a former college friend of the then US President Woodrow Wilson. In Spetember 1915, Dr. Sampson set out on a fishing trip into the Colorado gorges.

Days passed without his return. As a result, federal agents were ordered to search for him and indeed one of the largest man-hunts in history was initiated. The search for the missing man lasted for days, until apparently it was interrupted by the entrance of America to the 1st World War.

His disappearance was left behind – that was, until one day in July 1932, 17 years after he disappeared, when a ranger in the Rocky Mountains National Park came upon a skeleton 'to whose ribs fragments of clothing were still attached.'

Close by the skeleton was a diary. The diary belonged to the missing man. The location in which his skeleton and diary were found 'were in a very lonely part of Estes Park, and the remains lay at the foot of a cliff above the shores of Odessa Lake. One leg was fractured, and it was theorized that he had fallen from a high ledge, lain unconscious for hours, and died of exposure. But,' Watkins comments, 'one may ask: what was a fisherman doing on a high ledge in a canyon?' That's a good question. Having gone fishing, how had he got to the top of the cliff to fall off it? And why...?

~~~~

If you have experienced something strange & unusual, that's hard to explain, please feel free to let me know at www.stephyoungauthor.com I'm actively continuing to research and would be very interested.

I have a Podcast: Unexplained Mysteries with Steph Young on iTunes
https://itunes.apple.com/gb/podcast/unexplained-mysteries-bestselling-author-researcher/id1216208205?mt=2
or for Exclusive Episodes;
please go to Patreon.com Steph Young Podcast
https://www.patreon.com/stephyoungpodcast
Please go to StephYoungAuthor.com if you would like to subscribe to my mailing list, to stay up to date with new releases.

I hope you have enjoyed this book. If you have enjoyed it, perhaps you would be kind enough to leave a review, so that others too may learn of the most frightening and mysterious unexplained disappearances.

Thank you so much,
Steph

Also by Steph Young:

Stalked in the Woods

Demons: True Stories

True Stories of Real Time Travelers

Haunted Asylums

Creepy Tales of Unexplained Disappearances

Panic in the Woods

Unexplained Disappearances & Mysterious Deaths

Predators in the Woods

Desolating Spirits

An investigation into the Horrifying Case of 'The Smiley Face Killers.'

And many more ...

https://www.amazon.com/Steph-Young/e/B00KE8B6B0/

Printed in Great Britain
by Amazon

82176319R00149